THE
NEW TESTAMENT

NOTES

including
- *Introduction*
- *Historical Background of the* New Testament
- *Outline of the Life of Jesus*
- *Summaries and Commentaries*
- *Selected Bibliography*

D0390054

by
Charles H. Patterson, Ph.D.
Department of Philosophy
University of Nebraska

INCORPORATED

LINCOLN, NEBRASKA 68501

Editor

Gary Carey, M.A.
University of Colorado

Consulting Editor

James L. Roberts, Ph.D.
Department of English
University of Nebraska

ISBN 0-8220-0880-7
© Copyright 1965
by
Cliffs Notes, Inc.
All Rights Reserved
Printed in U.S.A.

1997 Printing

Cliffs Notes, Inc.   Lincoln, Nebraska

CONTENTS

> "There is no book in the English language that
> we quote oftener and understand less than we
> do the New Testament."
>
> **— Kee and Young**
> *Understanding the New Testament*

THE NEW TESTAMENT

FOREWORD

There is no single book that has influenced the course of Western civilization more than the New Testament. This in itself is sufficient reason for saying that some familiarity with its contents as well as appreciation of their worth is an essential element in what is generally known as a liberal education. Like other great books of the world its full meaning and significance cannot be grasped all at once. It requires something more than a rapid reading of the text and there is no short and easy way to acquire an adequate understanding of it. Certainly this little book of notes is not intended to provide the means for doing this nor should it be regarded as a substitute for studying the text itself. Its purpose is rather to provide some guidance for the student who wants to study the New Testament himself but who feels at a loss to know how to go about it. There are numerous questions which he feels must be answered before he is prepared to begin the study. Should he start reading it without any knowledge of the background from which it came into existence? Should the various writings be read in the order in which they are now arranged? Would it be better to study them in the chronological order in which they were written? Should an attempt be made to harmonize the writings with one another or should each one be considered by itself? Would a topical approach in which all of the materials having to do with a particular subject are assembled together have a particular advantage? Should one regard the New Testament as a divine book, a human book, or a combination of the two? These questions along with many others of a similar nature are pertinent to the study of the New Testament and the way in which they are answered will have an important bearing on the outcome. It is hoped that these notes will be helpful toward providing the best possible answers to them.

Books about the New Testament have been written from many different angles and it is possible to gain much valuable information from them. But the number and variety of these books often constitute a source of bewilderment unless one is guided in his selection of them. These notes are intended to be helpful in this respect although their primary purpose is to stimulate the student to read and to think for himself. No attempt is made here to force upon the reader any particular point of view or to tell him what he ought to believe about the New Testament. In the final analysis that is something which the student must do for himself. However, in doing this he should bear in mind that it is his responsibility to do it correctly or at least to come as close to that goal as he can. This means that in order for his interpretation to have any lasting value or permanent significance it must be formulated in the light of relevant facts and with due regard for consistency both with reference to itself and any known facts. If these notes can contribute something toward this end their purpose will then be achieved.

INTRODUCTION

The New Testament is a collection of writings in which different persons have set forth their convictions concerning the meaning and significance of the earthly career of Jesus of Nazareth. No one of these writings appeared until some years after Jesus had died. He left no written records concerning himself and any information about him must be gained from what other people have written. By the end of the first century of the Christian era, or thereabouts, several biographies of Jesus were written and four of these are now a part of the New Testament. Before any of these biographies were written Christian communities or what was later known as churches had been established and letters were sent to them for the purpose of instructing the members concerning the Christian way of life and telling them how to deal with local problems that had arisen in their midst. Some of these letters were written by a man named Paul who though he had been brought up in the strict traditions of the Jewish religion had been converted to Christianity and who spent the remainder of his life as a missionary founding new churches and nurturing the members in their newly acquired faith. After his death other leaders of the movement continued to write letters to churches and in this way they hoped to strengthen the organization and prepare its followers for any emergency which might arise. As the number of Christians increased and their influence came to be felt in various parts of the then known world opposition to the movement came from different quarters. Some of it came from the Jews who deeply resented the fact that many of their own people were forsaking Judaism and becoming Christians. The most severe opposition came from the Roman government which tried in various ways to suppress if not to annihilate the whole Christian movement on the grounds that it constituted a danger and a threat to the security of the empire.

When persecution of the Christians became extreme, messages were sent to them by leaders in the church. These messages were usually in the form of letters or public addresses. Their purpose was to encourage the ones who were suffering and to advise them concerning the way in which they should respond to the demands which were being made upon them.

Some of these messages are now a part of the New Testament. Other letters were written to counteract false doctrines that had arisen within the churches and several of these have been preserved. It is well, however, to bear in mind that none of these writings were intended by their respective authors to be regarded as sacred literature comparable to the Law and the Prophets of the Old Testament. Eventually, Christians did come to think of them in this way but the transition from a collection of writings designed originally to meet certain local problems to the status of sacred scriptures either replacing or else being added to the Old Testament required a comparatively long period of time. There are twenty-seven of these writings in the New Testament today. These were selected from a larger list of writings and it was not until the fourth century of our era that any general agreement was reached among the Christian churches as to the exact number and selection of writings which should be included. It is true that the Gospels and the letters of Paul were generally accepted prior to that time but there were other writings concerning which their inclusion in the canon of sacred scriptures was a matter of serious controversy.

In view of these facts it becomes obvious that an adequate understanding of any of the books in the New Testament cannot be obtained apart from some knowledge of the historical background from which they were written. Just how this knowledge can be obtained presents something of a problem. Our chief source of information is the New Testament itself. It is true that this is not our only source for there are some references to Jesus and the Christian movement in Roman history and in Jewish literature pertaining to the period in which he lived. But these non-Christian sources are very meager and we have good reasons for believing they were somewhat biased. Christian sources were no doubt biased too but in the case of both Christian and non-Christian sources we know the direction in which each of them is biased and we can make proper allowances for them. Since it is only in the Christian sources that we have any detailed account of the life and teachings of Jesus and the general character of the early Christian movement we need to center our attention on them.

It is in the New Testament biographies of Jesus, usually known as the four Gospels that we find the most extensive records of what Jesus did and of what he taught. But it is also in connection with these same biographies that the student of the New Testament encounters one of his difficult problems. How are these records to be evaluated? To what extent do they reveal what actually happened and to what extent do they merely indicate what the author believed to have happened? It will not do to answer these questions by asserting that these are all inspired writings and are therefore infallible in every respect. Divine inspiration is always and necessarily a two-fold process involving both a giving and a receiving. The giving may well be regarded as the divine part but the receiving or the understanding of whatever it is that has been revealed is the human part and that which is human is never infallible. Anyone who is at all sympathetic with the meaning and message of the New Testament will not be hesitant about regarding it as a divinely inspired book but if he is intellectually honest he will also recognize that there is a human element involved in the receiving and interpretation of that revelation. It is the human element which one must try to understand first for this is the medium through which the divine element must be communicated.

The human element which is present in the Gospel accounts is necessarily conditioned by the circumstances under which they were written. Since they were not written until approximately forty years after the death of Jesus they must be viewed from the perspective of the conditions which prevailed at that time. It is important to remember in this connection that the Christian community had been in existence for a considerable period of time. It came into existence because a group of people believed that the man Jesus who had been crucified was the long looked for Messiah. They were convinced that his life had met with divine approval and his death was not the result of any wrongdoing on his part. He had died for a righteous cause and in so doing he had achieved victory over the forces of evil for he had not yielded to any of their temptations in order to save himself. He was, in their judgment, the Messiah about whom the Old Testament prophets had spoken. By the time the Gospels were written stories which had been preserved orally by those who had been associated with Jesus were now viewed in the light of more recent events and interpreted in accordance with the beliefs which had become firmly established in the minds of the biographers. To reconstruct the original stories as they existed prior to the later interpretations placed upon them has been one of the main tasks of what is known as "form criticism." Although the methods used for this purpose have their limitations they are of value as a means toward understanding the New Testament.

The letters written by the Apostle Paul constitute nearly one-third of the New Testament. They were written long before any of the Gospels which we have now were in existence. Paul evidently knew something about the life of Jesus although he had not seen him in the flesh. His information, so far as we can determine, must have been obtained from the oral traditions which had been passed on to him by those who had been associated with him. Paul reports very little concerning the teachings of Jesus but his interpretation of the life, death, and resurrection of Jesus has had a profound influence on Christian history. The remaining portions of the New Testament while concerned primarily with specific problems and situations do nevertheless reflect the generally accepted beliefs concerning Jesus which were current among Christians at that time. Written accounts of what Jesus did during the course of his life were not considered necessary by the earliest Christians. They believed he would return to earth and establish the messianic kingdom in the very near future. Until that time the memories of his disciples and friends would be sufficient to preserve his deeds and his teachings. It was not until many of those who had been associated with him had died that the need for written records came to be recognized. After all that is included in our New Testament had been written it was some time before the manuscripts were assembled in their present form and used along with the Old Testament scriptures in the worship services of the Christian churches. Their status as inspired writings which were authoritative for the establishment of doctrines came about in response to a whole series of situations which developed within the Christian movement.

There are several different ways in which the study of the New Testament may be pursued. While there are benefits which may be derived from any one of them it does not follow that one method is as good as any other one. A brief statement with reference to various methods should make this clear. For example, one may begin by reading the books of the New Testament in the order in which they are now assembled. This will mean that one reads first of all the Gospel of Matthew. This was not the first Gospel to be written. It was placed first in the New Testament because it was regarded as the most important of the Gospels. Understanding the contents of this Gospel is difficult if not impossible until one sees it in relation to the other Gospels and to the historical situation from which it was produced. One needs to know the sources from which the author obtained his materials and the scheme which he followed in their selection and organization. It is also essential to know the purpose which he had in mind and the way in which his materials were used for the accomplishment of that purpose. Elements of the Gospel which appear to be in conflict with one another can scarcely be understood until one becomes familiar with the background from which each of them was derived. These difficulties along with many others are necessarily involved in the use of this method.

Another way of studying the New Testament consists in putting together all of the material found in any of the writings on a given subject. If this could be done successfully one might speak about the New Testament teaching on such subjects as money, divorce, Sabbath observance, spiritual gifts, and many other topics. Aside from the fact that an enquiry of this kind would be practically endless because of the number of topics that are mentioned, there is the more serious difficulty of fitting together the statements made by different persons under different circumstances and from different points of view. Nor can it be assumed without evidence to support it that different writers thought alike about any given subject.

Studying the books in the chronological order in which they were written does have some advantages in that it enables one to trace more directly the development of Christian thought through the period during which the New Testament was in the making. The chief objection to this method lies in the fact that Christianity was a going concern before any portion of the New Testament was written. The literature which it contains was the product of the Christian movement rather than the cause of it. It is for this reason that an understanding of what was written presupposes a certain familiarity with what had taken place before the writing began. When Paul wrote his letters to the Christian churches of his day he was writing to people who already knew something about the life of Jesus and the significance of what he had done. This, they must have obtained from oral traditions, because the sources from which we derive our information about him had not been written. Hence, it is necessary for us to consult the later literature of the New Testament in order to understand what was known earlier. In the case of the Gospels and other portions of the literature it is quite impossible to comprehend what the respective authors were saying apart from the beliefs which they were trying to establish.

In view of these considerations it seems wise to begin the study of the New Testament with a survey of the historical background which is implicit in the literature itself. This will necessarily include a brief survey of some of the more important elements in the religious life of the Jewish people prior to the beginning of the Christian era. It must also include an account of the religious hopes and ideals that were current among the Gentile or non-Jewish parts of the population. Some familiarity with both of these backgrounds is a prerequisite for the study of the New Testament for while Christianity had its earliest beginnings among the Jews it was not long until it began to spread among the Gentiles. For each of these groups its meaning had to be formulated in terms of the ideas and concepts to which they were accustomed. Knowing something about the religious beliefs and practices of these two groups together with the more pertinent facts in connection with the life of Jesus as it was understood by the early Christians prepares one for a more intelligent reading of the literature included in our New Testament.

THE HISTORICAL BACKGROUND OF
THE NEW TESTAMENT

The Christian churches of the first century drew their membership from both Jews and Gentiles. The first Christians had been Jews and their first missionary activities had been directed toward winning members from this group. It was not long, however, before their activities were extended to include Gentiles and many of those who had been non-Jews were welcomed into the newly formed Christian communities. The common element which was shared by both those who had been Jews and those who had been Gentiles was loyalty to the person known as Jesus of Nazareth. Both groups recognized him as a man of God and they looked forward to a time when the message which he had proclaimed would be spread throughout the world bringing salvation to all those who would receive it. But while both groups were loyal to this person they did not as a rule interpret his life and ministry in the same way. It could not reasonably be expected that they would. Each group found it necessary to interpret him in terms of the religious concepts with which they had long been familiar. For those who had been reared in the Jewish faith he was the Messiah, the anointed one, the chosen of God, about whom the Old Testament prophets had written. He was the one under whose guidance and leadership the kingdom of God would be established thus bringing about the full realization of the divine purpose in history. But while the Messiahship of Jesus meant a great deal to those whose training had been in Judaism it meant very little to the non-Jews or Gentiles. They were accustomed to think of religion in terms of the ideas and concepts associated with the mystery religions. To them Jesus was comparable to the heroic redeemer of the mystery cults. These cults were numerous in the Graeco-Roman world of New Testament times. Members of these cults were concerned primarily with the idea of salvation from physical death to be followed by participation in the life of another world which would be free of all the trials and hardships so characteristic of this present life. It was the chief function of the heroic redeemer to bring this about. It was believed that he would be a heavenly being who would descend to earth and after a life of service and self-sacrifice he would rise from the dead. By achieving a mystical union with him his followers would likewise gain the power to triumph over death. For many of the Christians who had been Gentiles it seemed perfectly natural to think of Jesus as one who had fulfilled the role of the heroic redeemer and it was on this basis that they accepted him. The different conceptions of Jesus which are found in the various writings of the New Testament can be understood only in the light of the different backgrounds from which they were developed.

THE JEWISH BACKGROUND

Christianity began with the belief that Jesus of Nazareth was the Messiah. He could not have been the Messiah if no one had believed he was the Messiah and the belief would not have occurred unless the Messiah had been expected. Hence the origin and development of the messianic idea among the Hebrew people has an important bearing on the literature of the New Testament. As far back as the eighth century B.C. the prophets of the Old Testament had expressed their conviction that some day a leader would arise in their midst and under his guidance a kingdom of justice and righteousness would be established here on this earth. During the centuries which followed this belief was modified in various ways but it was never completely abandoned. Three different stages can be noted in the development of the messianic idea. The first one may be designated as *prophetic* messianism. The other two are known respectively as *apocalyptic* messianism and *revolutionary* messianism. All three had to do with the establishment on earth of the kingdom of God. This was regarded as the ultimate goal of history or the final realization of the divine purpose in regard to the destiny of the human race. The three types of messianism differed with one another in respect to the time and manner of its accomplishment. Prophetic messianism taught that this goal would be reached with the coming of the Messiah or anointed one. It was believed that he would be an actual king who would reign over the Israelite nation and so direct its affairs that the evils in society would be overcome and peace and happiness would be the lot of all.

When Saul was chosen to be the first king of Israel we are told that he was anointed with oil by the prophet Samuel in the presence of a multitude of people. This was an important ceremony for it symbolized the hope that this "anointed one" would be the Messiah under whose leadership the divine purpose would be realized. Saul's reign did not turn out very well and when things were going rather badly David was anointed to be king in place of Saul. David's reign was in many respects more successful. Later generations looked back upon it as a kind of golden age in the history of the Israelite people. The hope for the coming of the Messiah was emphasized more and more in the teachings of the prophets. Because so many of Israel's actual kings had been so disappointing in what they did the prophets talked about the coming of an ideal king who would appear in the future and do for his people that which other kings had been unable to do. This king, it was said, would be like King David. Later on it was maintained that he would be a descendant from the line of David. This idea is expressed in the writings of the prophet Isaiah.

The course of Hebrew history over the centuries did not bring about a fulfillment of their hopes. Instead, one disaster after another overtook the nation. After the death of King Solomon, Israel was divided into a northern and a southern kingdom. Each of these went through a series of tragic experiences. In 722 B.C. the northern kingdom was taken into captivity by the Assyrians. A century and a half later the southern kingdom suffered a similar fate at the hands of the Babylonians. Eventually a Hebrew state was restored for a time but conditions were far from ideal. Internal strife was present and the nation was under a constant threat of destruction by foreign enemies. Under these conditions prophetic messianism began to wane and a new type known as apocalyptic messianism appeared in its place.

The dominant characteristic of this new type was a conviction that the kingdom of God would not come about by a gradual transformation of society under the leadership of a great and good king. Rather, it would be brought about by a sudden supernatural intervention. When the right time arrived God would act bringing punishment to all the forces of evil and establish his kingdom as a dwelling place for the righteous for all time to come. This event was referred to as the coming of the "day of the Lord." It was described as a great catastrophic event, an end of the world, and the ushering in of a new age. Although there are variations in the different apocalyptic writings some of them convey the idea that the Messiah will be a heavenly being who will descend to earth and inaugurate the new era. His appearance will bring destruction to the wicked and deliverance to the righteous. There will be a resurrection of the dead and a judgment of all the people who have lived on the earth. After the wicked have been completely destroyed there will be a new heaven and a new earth in which only justice and righteousness will prevail.

Apocalyptic messianism was especially meaningful in times of crisis and for the Jews this meant most of the time. The book of Daniel in the Old Testament was written primarily for those who were suffering persecution from the Syrians under Antiochus Epiphanes during the period which preceded the Maccabean wars. In New Testament times it was the Roman government which persecuted the Christians and the book of Revelations did for the Christians of that day what the book of Daniel did for the Jews of an earlier date. In both instances the message conveyed had a similar import. It assured those who were suffering for their faith that although the evil forces in the world were then in the ascendancy the time was not far distant when God would intervene bringing an end to the reign of evil and establishing a kingdom of righteousness in which those who had proved faithful through all of their trials and afflictions would dwell in peace forever.

Not all of the Jews were satisfied with the notion that they should endure suffering and persecution while waiting for God in his own good time to intervene in their behalf. The *revolutionary* messianists argued that God would come to their aid only after they had done all that they could for themselves. Accordingly, they believed that the "Day of the Lord" would be hastened if they would take up arms against their enemies and fight for their own freedom and independence. In other words God would use his own people as the instruments through which he would bring punishment upon the unrighteous nations. The belief that God would aid them in doing this was strengthened by what they had experienced during the period of the Maccabean wars. When Mattathias and his little band of renegade fighters took up arms against the Syrians they actually achieved one remarkable victory after another. In spite of the fact that they were greatly outnumbered by Syrian soldiers they were able to win back the territory that had been taken from them. They regained possession of the city of Jerusalem and restored the worship services of the Temple. All of this was interpreted to mean that God would protect them in battle and give them victory over their enemies. What he had done for them in times past he would do again if they would only follow a similar course. After the Romans had conquered Palestine and made the Jews subjects of their dominion, revolutionary messianists continued their efforts by calling upon Jews to launch a revolt against the government of Rome. Not long before the birth of Jesus of Nazareth, a certain Judas of Galilee claiming the messianic role for himself had organized a revolt which the Romans had put down with unmistakable cruelty. It was this fear of rebellion which made the Romans suspicious whenever it was rumored that a Jewish Messiah had appeared among his people.

Another important characteristic of Judaism can be seen in their conception of the Law and its relation to the conduct of people. According to their tradition the Law was from God. It had been revealed to Moses and through him it had been communicated to the entire Israelite nation. Because God was the author of the Law it was believed that the precepts contained in it were binding for all time to come. The Law was as unchangeable as God himself. The Law included not only the ten commandments but all the statutes and ordinances found in the "Book of the Law" or what is now recognized as the first five books of the Old Testament. Many of these laws were no doubt added to the original codes long after the death of Moses. Nevertheless, tradition had attributed all of them to Moses and taken as a whole they constituted for the orthodox Jew the standard of righteousness according to which not only the people who were living then but all succeeding generations would be judged. Obedience with reference to the laws which God had commanded was the measure of goodness. This being true it was a matter of great importance to know exactly what the requirements of the law were and how these were to be applied to particular cases. This was not always an easy matter to determine for instances would occur where different laws would appear to be in conflict and one would be at a loss to know just which one he ought to follow. One of the main tasks of the Scribes was to determine matters of this kind. It was their job to state precisely the conditions under which a given law would be applicable. Frequently it would become necessary for them to state when exceptions should be made to certain laws. Further than this, occasions would arise when they would have to make exceptions to these exceptions. It was a very complicated and confusing process. Nevertheless it was an important one for if a person was to be judged solely on the basis of whether he had obeyed the law there must be some authoritative way of knowing exactly what the law required under a given set of circumstances. It may be remembered that throughout the Gospels of the New Testament the chief accusation brought by the Jews against Jesus was that he was a law-breaker.

Although Judaism is often referred to as a single type of religious belief and practice it would be a mistake to suppose there was complete agreement among all the Jews concerning either doctrine or manner of living. We can in fact distinguish several sects or parties within Judaism itself. It will be sufficient for our purpose to mention a few of the more important ones. The largest and most influential of these sects was known as the *Pharisees.* They were the ones who took their religion most seriously. This was especially true with reference to their attitude toward the Law. They believed the Jews were God's chosen people, distinguished from all others by the fact that God had revealed his standard of goodness to them, and they alone were the ones who lived in conformity with it. Their zeal for the Law made them appear exclusive and self-righteous to those who did not belong to their group. They avoided contact with foreigners and their customs so far as it was possible for them to do so. They were especially antagonistic toward the influences derived from the culture of the Greeks and the Romans. Their motive was to avoid contamination with the evil ways of the world. They believed in a life after death in which the righteous would be rewarded and the sinners punished for the deeds which they had committed. In many parts of the New Testament the Pharisees are severely criticized but we need to bear in mind that these accounts were written by people who did not belong to their group. Without doubt the accounts given are accurate with reference to some of the Pharisees but it would be a mistake to think they were all like that. Many of them were men of the finest character representing in some instances Judaism at its very best.

The *Sadducees* were another sect, smaller in number than the Pharisees, but very influential in determining the policies which affected the life of the people as a whole. In some respects they were a conservative group for they held a strict and literal interpretation of the written Law as it was recorded in the Torah or the first five books of the Old Testament. They rejected the so-called oral law which consisted of the comments and interpretations of prominent rabbis made over long periods of time. Neither did they take seriously many of the ideas presented in the later books of the Old Testament. For example, they did not believe in the resurrection of the dead as it is set forth in the book of Daniel. But in their attitude toward Hellenic culture and Roman law they were far more liberal than the Pharisees. They took the position that while some important truths had been revealed to the Jews other nations had an important contribution to make as well. This being true they advocated an intermingling of the various cultures of their day thus giving to each group the opportunity of an enrichment of their own understanding through contact with others. Because the priesthood was in the hands of the Sadducees and the appointments made had to be confirmed by officials of the civil government this sect was able to exercise political power. Sometimes this power was used more to promote selfish interests than for the benefit of the people as a whole.

A third sect was known as the *Essenes*. It was this group that produced the famous Dead Sea Scrolls which were discovered in recent times. From these scrolls much has been learned concerning the history of the period which preceded the writings which make up the New Testament. The Essenes were a group of Jews who were seriously disturbed by the way things were going in and around the city of Jerusalem. It seemed to them that the religion of the fathers proclaimed by priests and prophets of old had ceased to have any meaningful relation to the lives of the people. They saw so much wickedness in the society around them that they felt impelled to move away from it all and live in a secluded colony where they would be sheltered from the evils of the day. In this respect their attitude was similar to that of the medieval monks of later generations who withdrew from a worldly society in order to live a holier type of life. At first the Essenes like the later monks advocated celibacy hoping to maintain their numbers by adding new converts to their order. Later, marriages were permitted but the people of both sexes were required to conform to a very rigid set of disciplinary rules. They were a communistic society sharing their goods with one another and making spiritual preparations for the end of the world and the setting up of the messianic kingdom which they expected to take place in the near future. Much of their time was spent in study and in copying the manuscripts of the Old Testament writings. Besides the works which they copied the Essenes produced a considerable amount of literature of their own, some of which describes their manner of living along with the rites and ceremonies which they observed.

Besides these three sects which we have mentioned there were other smaller and less influential groups. One of these was known as the *Zealots*. They were revolutionary messianists who believed in the use of violent methods in order to gain freedom from their oppressors. They were feared by the Romans because of their tendency to stir up rebellion against the recognized government. We read in the New Testament that one of the twelve disciples whom Jesus chose was Simon the Zealot. The *Zadokites* were reformed priests who resented the way in which the Sadducees had made political offices out of the priesthood. They believed in the religious ideals which had been advocated by the great prophets of the Old Testament and they tried as best they could to make these effective. They produced some of the apocalyptic literature to which Paul made reference in one of his letters to the Thessalonians. The comparatively large number of people who belonged to the poorer classes were known as the *Am'ha'aretz* or people of the land. They were the manual laborers who performed the more menial tasks of the day. They were, to some extent, held in contempt by the Pharisees and Sadducees who considered themselves morally superior to these persons whose hard lot they believed was precisely what they deserved because of their laxity in the observance of ritualistic requirements of the Law. It was from this class of discouraged and oppressed persons that Jesus drew many of his followers. They are referred to in the Gospels which tell us "the common people heard him gladly."

THE NON-JEWISH BACKGROUND

Early Christianity made its appeal to Gentiles as well as to those who had been Jews. Consequently the books of the New Testament reflect something of their background along with that of the Israelite people. It is of course impossible to do more than mention a few of the more important influences which have a direct bearing on the literature produced by the early Christians. For a more extensive account one should consult any of the standard works in this field. The Gentile version of Christianity was influenced by many different factors, three of which we will describe briefly. They are the *Mystery cults, Emperor worship,* and *Greek philosophy.*

The mystery cults were secret organizations with membership restricted to those who had made application for admittance and who had passed through a probationary period during which their conduct had been carefully observed by qualified officials. Unless they had performed the necessary rites and met all of the specified tests they were not allowed to become members. There were many mystery cults throughout the Graeco-Roman world during New Testament times. They include the

Eleusinian Mysteries, the *Orphic Mysteries,* the *Attis-Adonis Mysteries,* the *Isis-Osiris Mysteries, Mithraism,* and many others. The actual ceremonies which took place within any of these cults were supposed to be kept secret. However, there are certain general characteristics of the mystery religions which are fairly well known. All of them were concerned primarily with the means of obtaining salvation. They believed that life in this present world was so infected with evil that no permanent good could be achieved in it. Consequently, salvation for them meant getting out of this world and entering into a new type of existence in a life which comes after one's physical death. Each of the mystery cults had its own peculiar mythology which described in some detail the activities of the gods that were involved. Many of the myths appear to have had their origin in an attempt to explain the change of seasons which causes the death of vegetation in the fall of the year and its rebirth in the spring. As the mythology developed the death and resurrection which occurs in the vegetable kingdom came to be regarded as an appropriate symbol of what can happen in the lives of human beings. Since it was through the power of the gods that vegetation overcomes death, it was believed that mankind through the aid of a supernatural power might also triumph over death. The agent through whom this power would be made available was known as the *heroic redeemer.* Unlike the Jewish concept of the Messiah whose function was that of establishing a kingdom of justice and righteousness on this earth, the heroic redeemer of the mystery cults was a savior who was able to conquer death not only for himself but for all of his faithful followers. He was a heavenly being who would come to earth in human form and who would use his miraculous power to perform deeds of mercy and kindness toward human beings. His work would encounter opposition from the forces of evil and his earthly career would be brought to an end by a sacrificial death. By virtue of his power as a divine being he would rise from the dead and ascend back to the heaven from whence he came.

The power that was manifest in the experiences of the heroic redeemer could be imparted to the members of the cult who were prepared to receive it. It was in order to prepare them for this experience that the applicants for membership were required to go through certain initiatory rites. These usually included a sprinkling ceremony in which either water or blood would be used thus signifying a purifying process which would cleanse the individual of his evil ways. After the applicant became a member there were other ceremonies designed to bring about a mystical union between the believer and his redeemer. In one of these ceremonies the initiates would be seated in front of a stage where they would witness a dramatic performance which would portray the life, death, and resurrection of the redeemer. As they would see this drama enacted they would feel a sense of kinship with the hero. Being united in spirit with him they, too, would possess the power to overcome the evils of mortal existence including even death itself. In another type of ceremony, union with the redeemer would be accomplished through participation in a common meal. Here the members of the cult would gather around a table and partake in a symbol of the body and blood of the redeemer, believing that in this way the life that was present in him would be imparted to them. Membership in the cult and participation in its many rites and ceremonies was regarded as an essential means for transforming the quality of one's living on this earth in preparation for his true salvation which would be achieved in a life to come after death.

Emperor worship was another factor which had an important bearing on the religious life of the Gentile world. Its chief significance lies in the concept of a human being who in the course of time is elevated in the minds of his followers to the status of deity. In other words a man becomes a god. This was a way of thinking which stands in sharp contrast with that of the Jews. Judaism always made a sharp distinction between the human and the divine. Yahweh, the god of the Jewish religion, was regarded as the Creator and in a sense the father of all mankind. But he was not a father in any physical or biological sense of the term. Human beings were born of two human parents but not of one human parent and one divine parent. This was not always the case among other peoples of the world. Among non-Jews the concept of an individual who has one human parent and one divine parent was fairly common. To be sure it was only the exceptional individual whose earthly career would be explained in this way and the most frequent example of it was found in the ruler of a country. One way of accounting for the extraordinary achievements of the head of a government was to credit him with supernatural ancestry on the grounds that no ordinary human being born in the usual way could have accomplished so much. Having a divine parent was interpreted to mean that the individual belonged to the race of the gods and was therefore not comparable to ordinary mortals. The so-called deification of a ruler did not always take place during his lifetime. After his death later generations would idealize both his reign and his person, thus giving rise to the belief that he was something more than a man. This happened in the case of the Greek ruler who came to be known as Alexander the Great and again among the Romans who likewise deified Julius Ceasar. One of the most revered of the Roman emperors was Augustus Caesar. After his death he was declared by the Roman senate to have been a god and worship of his image was encouraged in various parts of the empire. Not only was he deified in the minds of his admirers of later generations but legends indicating his supernatural character came into existence and were given wide publicity. It was reported that his birth had been foretold by a heavenly messenger, strange phenomena had been observed in the heavens at the time of his birth, miraculous power had been manifested in many of his earthly activities, and finally he had even triumphed over death. We have the testimony of one Roman historian who claimed that eye witnesses had told of his resurrection from the dead and his ascension into heaven.

The deification of earthly rulers by their subjects was not confined to the Greeks and the Romans. It had for centuries been a common practice among Egyptians, Babylonians, and other peoples of the ancient world. Nor were the rulers the only ones who had been deified by their followers. Some of the most noted of the Greek philosophers were said to have descended from the gods since their remarkable wisdom could be accounted for in no other way. Among the Gentiles of New Testament times it was not at all uncommon for explanations of this kind to be given to account for the activities of a person who had accomplished extraordinary things.

By the end of the first century of the Christian era, emperor worship led to a serious conflict between officials of the Roman government and the members of Christian communities. Certain of the Roman emperors in order to strengthen their prestige and establish further unity among their subjects had decided that their deification should not be postponed until later generations would bring it about. Accordingly, they not only proclaimed their own deity but gave orders that statues in their honor should be erected in the provinces and worship should be accorded them at specified times and places. Christians were thus placed in an embarrassing position. To refuse to conform to the orders of the emperor would brand them as enemies of the civil government while obeying these same orders would be an act of disloyalty to the one and only God whom they recognized. Portions of the New Testament were addressed to Christians who were faced with this dilemma and who needed both advice and encouragement with reference to the course which they should follow.

The influence of *Greek philosophy* was widespread throughout the Graeco-Roman world. The Greek language was used by educated people, and Greek schools of philosophy were established in leading cities of the Roman empire. The writings of the Old Testament had been translated into Greek by the seventy scholars whose work was known as the *Septuagint* version of the Hebrew scriptures. The influence of Greek ideas can be seen in many instances of New Testament writing, especially in those parts of the literature in which an attempt is being made to interpret the Christian religion of people whose prior experience had been in a Gentile rather than a Jewish environment. This was true to a considerable extent of the Pauline letters and also of the Gospel of John. In both of these instances the writings were addressed to communities which were composed of Gentile as well as Jewish Christians. It was therefore necessary for these authors to use language with which the people to whom they were writing were familiar and could readily understand. Greek influences can be noted too in other parts of the New Testament although they are not as conspicuous there as they are in the writings of Paul and John.

It would be hard to say just how much of the New Testament was influenced either directly or indirectly by Greek conceptions but there are at least three areas in which they can be recognized readily. These include the doctrine of the *Logos* which may be translated as *Word* or *Reason,* ethical conceptions having to do with the conflict between flesh and spirit, and the belief in immortality.

When the author of the fourth Gospel, commonly known as the Gospel of John began his account of Christianity by saying "In the beginning was the Word, and the Word was with God, and the Word was God" he was using a concept which had long been familiar to students of Greek philosophy. The Word or *Logos* which was the term used by the Greeks has a long and interesting history. One finds it in the writings of Heracleitus, one of the Pre-Socratics whose work appears to have had considerable influence on the philosophies of Plato and of Aristotle. For Heracleitus the Logos was a kind of cosmic order or divine justice which presided over the destinies of a changing world. Whenever either of two opposite forces operative in the world would overstep its bounds the Logos would see to it that a proper balance was restored. Light and darkness, heat and cold, wet and dry, male and female, like all the other pairs of opposites would thus be kept in proper relation to one another. Nor was the work of the Logos confined to the physical aspect of nature. It had to do with the moral order as well. Whenever the requirements of justice would be violated either by individuals or by nations the Logos would act in a compensatory manner bringing punishment on the evildoers and thus restoring the proper balance of things. Plato regarded the Logos or Reason as the divine element which is present in human beings. Its demand for harmony among the elements included in human nature provided the key to the real meaning of the good life.

It was in Stoicism more than in any other branch of Greek philosophy that the doctrine of the Logos was emphasized. They identified Reason with God. They did not conceive of it as having an existence apart from the world but they held that it permeated every part of the world. It was by virtue of the Logos or Reason that the world was a cosmos rather than a chaos. Reason was present too in the mind of man. Knowledge was made possible because the rational element in human nature was akin to the reason which exists in nature, the only difference being that in the former case reason becomes conscious of itself. So far as humanity is concerned it is the function of reason to give guidance and direction to the activities of life. Because all men are rational beings there is a common bond between them and this was recognized by the Stoics as the basis for their belief in the universal brotherhood of man. It was reason operating in the lives of human beings that made possible the realization of what constituted for them the real meaning of the good life. The Stoic ideal was expressed in the words "life according to nature." This meant a life that was directed by the rational element which is present in both nature and man. It could be achieved by bringing one's feelings and desires under the control of reason. This they believed was a real possibility for any normal human being. Epictetus, one of the well known Stoic writers, described this way of life in an essay which he entitled "Things within our Power and Things not within our Power." The individual has power over his own inner attitudes. He can govern his own spirit. He can control his temper. He can follow the path of duty rather than yield to his feelings or be led by his emotions. On the other hand it was recognized that in the life of everyone circumstances arise over which he has no control. Some things that happen are inevitable and the wise man will accept them without fear or complaint. The Apostle Paul reflected this ideal when he wrote in one of his letters "I have learned in whatsoever state I am there to be content."

Closely related to the concept of the Logos or Divine Reason is the notion of conflict between flesh and spirit. This idea is one that pervades the whole structure of Greek philosophy. It is illustrated in the teachings of Plato who held that it was the world of ideas or the realm of the spirit which constitutes reality. This is the realm of the eternal or the unchanging. In contrast the world that is experienced through the senses is a changing and unstable one. We could not have any knowledge concerning it except for the unchanging ideas which participate in it. It is the presence of these ideas which are copied or imitated in particular things that gives to them the appearance of reality. But when ideas are embodied or imitated in material things the result is always somewhat inferior to the original. In other words matter is the source of corruption or deterioration.

Ideas conceived in this way were something more than a basis for the existence of particular things. They were also ideals or standards of perfection, thus making it possible for particular things to be evaluated in terms of their approximation of the ideal. To call an object a good object means that it is a close approximation to the ideal, one that is as nearly like the ideal as it is possible for a physical object to be. In a similar way of thinking a man is morally good when he conforms to the pattern of the ideal as much as it is possible for a human being to do. Centuries after Plato, Christians illustrated this point when they said of Jesus of Nazareth "The word was made flesh and dwelt among men." Jesus was regarded as an embodiment of the ideal. He was the ideal man, the standard according to which the goodness of any other human being was to be judged.

All of this means that for the Greeks the source of goodness is spirit and evil has its roots in matter. Because a human being is composed of both matter and spirit there is a struggle which is constantly going on within his own nature. The conflict between good and evil which takes place in the life of an individual is a conflict between the desires of the flesh and the demands of the reason which is the ruling part of one's spiritual nature. Now the idea of a good mind and an evil body which was characteristic of Greek philosophy was never accepted by the Jews. They taught that man was created in the image of God. Body, soul, and spirit constituted a unit and all of it was pronounced good. Evil came in with the fall of man and it infected all of the elements in his nature including the mind as well as the body. The Apostle Paul was brought up in the Jewish tradition and there is no indication that he ever abandoned the notion of original sin. Nevertheless, in writing to Gentile Christians he frequently used the language of Greek philosophy. For example in the letter to the Galatians he writes "This I say then, Walk in the Spirit, and ye shall not fulfill the lust of the flesh. For the flesh lusteth against the Spirit, and the Spirit against the flesh: and these are contrary the one to the other." And again he says, "Now the works of the flesh are manifest, which are these: adultery, fornication, uncleanness, etc." "But the fruit of the Spirit is love, joy, peace, longsuffering, etc."

The Greek conception of a good mind but an evil body is illustrated again in their teaching concerning the immortality of the soul. Unlike the. Hebrews who never accepted the idea of a soul existing apart from the body, Plato and many of his followers believed that souls have neither a beginning nor an end. They belong to the eternal realm of the spirit but they are capable of entering human bodies and remaining there until the body dies. During this time they can be influenced by their contact with that which is physical and as a result they may be dragged down toward the level of matter or they may so direct the physical body that its activities will be in the direction of spiritual attainments. In one of Plato's well known dialogues the career of the soul is described as being something like that of a charioteer who is driving two steeds, one of which is wild and unruly, while the other one behaves in an orderly manner. It is up to the charioteer to determine which one of these steeds will be subdued by the other. The two steeds represent the flesh and the spirit and the soul is the charioteer. The meaning of the simile is that the soul throughout the course of its embodied existence is engaged in a conflict between flesh and spirit which is also a conflict between good and evil. The souls which yield to the demands of the flesh are deserving of a different fate from those who follow the promptings of the spirit. This is one of the main reasons why Plato believed in the immortality of the soul. The souls which do not receive the happiness which they deserve in one life can be given a just compensation in another one. This provides a solution for the problem concerning the suffering of comparatively innocent persons. They may be receiving just punishment for deeds done in a former existence or it may be they will be given an appropriate reward in a future one.

Another reason for believing in the immortality of the soul lies in the fact that the ideas which are present in the soul have neither beginning nor end. They are eternal and therefore the soul in which they have their existence must possess a similar nature. On no other basis does he think it possible to account for the ideas which one can think but which are never experienced through the senses. One can think a perfect circle or a perfectly straight line although neither one has ever been seen. Plato's explanation is that the ideas have always been present in the soul. One's awareness of them is a recollection of what happened in some former existence. They are latent in the soul of a human being and are raised to the level of consciousness as a result of the stimulus provided by sensations.

When Plato writes his account of the death of Socrates he makes a clear distinction between what happens to the physical body and what happens to the soul. When friends come to the prison to be with him during his last hours Socrates explains that this is no occasion for sadness since the time has about arrived when his soul is to be released from the body in which it has been imprisoned for so many years. It is only the physical body that dies. The soul is about to go on its journey to another world unencumbered with the difficulties that have attended its existence in a mortal body. In this future existence the soul will receive a just reward for whatever goodness it has achieved, and since Socrates believes that he has lived well he looks to the future with joyful anticipation.

This conception of the soul and its relation to a life beyond physical death was widely held by the Gentiles of the Graeco-Roman world during New Testament times. It is true that neither the Jews nor the early Jewish Christians thought of it that way although many if not most of them did believe in some kind of a survival of physical death. We know that the early Christian movement was to a very great extent based on a firm belief in the resurrection of Jesus. As the story of this resurrection was told in various places it was not always interpreted in the same way. We can readily understand why this was true. Those whose orientation had been in the Greek tradition were bound to see in it something quite different from those who had been brought up in a Jewish environment.

A BRIEF OUTLINE OF THE
LIFE OF JESUS

Our information concerning the events in the life of Jesus is obtained almost entirely from the Gospels of the New Testament. It is necessary, however, for the student of these writings to bear in mind that before any of these Gospels were written the Christian community had been in existence for some time. Those who belonged to this community had formulated a number of specific beliefs concerning Jesus and the significance of his life, death, and resurrection. When the Gospels were written the materials contained in them necessarily reflected to a considerable extent those beliefs which were generally accepted by Christians at that time. Not only the specific beliefs but also their interpretation and significance for coming generations were bound to become a part of the biographies which they wrote. There is nothing strange or unusual about this for it is the kind of thing that is always involved in historical writing. Historians, to be sure, make use of source materials and they record actual happenings with as much accuracy as possible. Even so, it is their selection of facts that is recorded and it is their interpretation of them that governs the way in which they are put together. This is true of the New Testament writings no less than it is of other historical writings. The authors of the Gospels, inspired as they undoubtedly were, could not help but be influenced by the beliefs which they held about Jesus. It would have been most natural for them to fill in the gaps that would occur in their accounts by telling what they believed must have happened or even to insert at various points what seemed appropriate in the light of subsequent events. It is not always an easy task to determine just how much of the record as it exists at the present time is due to the interpretations of the authors nor can this be done with complete accuracy. So far as the main outline of events is concerned there is no reason for doubting their historical accuracy but like any other historical writing, appropriate allowances must be made for the limitations under which the different authors carried on their work.

The oldest of the biographies of Jesus which, according to most New Testament scholars is the Gospel of Mark, tells us nothing of the time or place of Jesus' birth nor does it record anything of his life prior to the time when he was baptized by John in the river Jordan. It may be that information concerning the early part of his life was not available or that it was not regarded as important. Other Gospels report that he was born in Bethlehem of Judea and that he grew up in the town of Nazareth in Galilee. His public ministry did not begin until after his baptism. This was apparently a turning point in his career. John the Baptist had been conducting a vigorous campaign in preparation for the great day which he believed to be near at hand when God would establish his kingdom here on earth. John called upon the people to repent of their sins and in witness thereof to be baptized. The fact that Jesus responded to this call and was baptized indicates that he was in full accord with the work John was doing. Shortly thereafter he too began to proclaim the coming of the kingdom and called upon his fellow men to make preparation for it. The work of John the Baptist was brought to a close when he was imprisoned and later beheaded by Herod Antipas. This may have been one of the reasons why Jesus continued, at least in part, the type of work which John had been doing although there are good reasons for believing he would have carried out a program of his own quite independent of what happened to the Baptist. Before beginning his own public ministry Jesus, like many of Israel's prophets, retired to the solitude of the wilderness for a period of fasting and meditation. At the end of this period we are told that he was tempted by Satan the arch enemy of God and the personification of the forces of evil. Although the details of the temptation stories are somewhat varied there can be little doubt that they report an actual event and the meaning of the experience is essentially the same in all of them. They tell us that this man was tempted to do evil in the manner which is typical of the temptations that come to all human beings. The fact that he was able with divine help to resist these temptations brings assurance to any other person that he too may overcome evil by cooperating with divine aid the same as Jesus did.

According to the Gospel of Mark, Jesus began his public ministry in the towns and villages of Galilee by proclaiming that the kingdom of God was at hand. He spoke in synagogues, in private homes, on the lake shore, or wherever people would gather to see and to hear him. Two elements in his ministry were so closely linked together that neither one can be understood apart from the other. They were teaching and healing. Both of them had to do with overcoming the forces of evil in preparation for the coming of the kingdom. The purpose of the preaching or teaching mission was to bring people to an awareness of their need for repentance and to give them a clearer understanding of the way they should live in order to be ready for a place in God's kingdom. One of the chief devices used by Satan to lead people astray was the development of a sense of complete satisfaction with themselves. This is what has often been designated as the sin of pride. It is a feeling on the part of individuals that they are already good enough and there is no need for any reform on their part. It was this aspect of Satan's work that he wanted to counteract and preaching was one of the means used to accomplish this end. The healing mission was another means employed for the same purpose. It was generally accepted by the Jewish people that physical suffering was in the main a punishment for sin. This point is well illustrated in the story concerning the healing of the man who was born blind. The first question put to Jesus by those who were standing nearby was "Who sinned, this man or his parents that he was born blind?" But if suffering was a punishment for sin then an assurance that one's sins had been forgiven would be followed by a removal of the punishment. The Gospel accounts all indicate that in Jesus' ministry the healing of the sick and the forgiveness of sins were so closely linked together that they were but different ways of reporting the same event. To overcome sickness as well as erroneous beliefs was to counteract the work of the evil one and thus to prepare for the coming of the kingdom.

According to the account in Mark the early ministry of Jesus in Galilee was quite successful. Large crowds of people gathered to hear him and many of those who were sick were brought to him in order that they might be cured. To assist him in the work he was doing, as well as to instruct them further concerning life in the kingdom, Jesus chose a group of disciples. They came from different walks of life and were so deeply impressed by the character of Jesus' mission that they wanted to be closely associated with it. This does not mean that they fully understood it. Apparently they all believed that the kingdom was soon to be established but they were not in complete agreement concerning the manner in which it would be brought about and there was some doubt in their minds with reference to the precise role of Jesus in connection with it. For a long time the Jews had believed that the coming of the Messiah would precede the establishment of the kingdom but there was some question in the minds of the disciples whether Jesus was the one who had long been expected. In Mark's Gospel Jesus' messiahship was a secret known only by Jesus himself and the demons whom he encountered. It was not revealed even to the disciples until he discussed it with them at Caesarea Philippi shortly before the journey to Jerusalem and then he warned them that they should say nothing about it.

We have no definite information concerning the length of Jesus' public ministry. So far as the events related in the Gospel of Mark are used as the basis for calculating it we can say that it would have been possible for all of them to have occurred within a single year. Other Gospels indicate a longer period of time. Whatever length of time it may have been it seems evident that the purpose of the ministry was only that of preparing the people for life in the kingdom. None of Jesus' mighty works were done in order to attract attention to himself. The miracles were manifestations of the power of God which was always available to those who were prepared to make use of it. To be sure there were some persons who saw in these miracles nothing more than a species of magic or the exhibition of some spectacular power but they were the ones who failed to grasp the true meaning or significance of his work.

At some point in his Galilean ministry Jesus had a disappointing experience in his home town of Nazareth. Concerning it, the remark is made "a prophet is without honor in his own country." It is also stated that Jesus could do no more mighty works in that place because of their unbelief. The experience did not dampen his enthusiasm for carrying forward the mission he had set out to perform. It merely intensified his efforts. He sent his disciples into the outlying territory with instructions to do the same type of work which he had been going. Their efforts appear to have been successful for when they brought back their report Jesus said with reference to it "I saw Satan fall as lightning from heaven." Later Jesus and the disciples carried their mission into the region northeast of Galilee including such places as Tyre, Sidon, and Caesarea Philippi. After a brief return to Galilee, in which he visited the city of Capernaum, he decided to go to Jerusalem. The growing opposition to his work on the part of those who were engaged in the activities which he criticized seems to have been one of the reasons which prompted this decision. But more than that was involved for the success of his entire mission was at stake and it was a matter of crucial importance that the cause which he represented should be placed squarely before the leaders of the Jewish people in their headquarters at Jerusalem. He realized the danger that was involved in an attempt of this kind for he was familiar with what had happened to Israel's ancient prophets whenever they challenged the policies being followed by the officials of their government. Nevertheless, in spite of all the dangers which might come to him personally, "he set his face steadfastly toward Jerusalem" no matter what it might cost him to do so. As he talked with his disciples about what might happen to him in Jerusalem they were shocked for they did not believe anything of that kind would happen to the promised Messiah. When Jesus tried to explain to them the true nature of the work of the Messiah they did not understand.

The journey to Jerusalem was relatively uneventful but after his entrance into the city it was not long until the opposition to his program became so strong that it ended in his death. His coming into the city is described by the Gospel writers as a triumphal entry for evidently there were many persons who welcomed his entry believing that the time was at hand when the promised Messiah would take part in the establishment of the kingdom. Their hopes were soon frustrated by the turn of events. The chief priests and rulers of the people were infuriated by his attacks on the use that was being made of the Temple. When he drove out the buyers and sellers and denounced the commercialism involved in their activities he aroused the antagonism of the Jewish leaders and this led to their decision to get rid of him. It was the season for the celebration of the Jewish Passover and multitudes would be coming into the city to participate in the services. Jesus observed the Passover meal with his disciples but in the meantime his enemies had plotted against him by charging that he was not only disloyal to the Jewish faith but an enemy of the Roman government. After the Passover meal he was betrayed by one of his own disciples and arrested by soldiers who had been sent out to take him. In the course of his trial before the Roman governor he was examined by Pilate who declared that he found in him no fault at all. Pilate wanted that he should be released but the mob that had gathered to press charges against him demanded that he be crucified, and in the end Pilate yielded to their demands. From the point of view of those who had been his followers it was indeed a dark day. It looked as though everything for which they had hoped was lost. Even the disciples forsook him and fled in order to save their own lives. He died on the cross and was buried in Joseph's new tomb.

Sometime later a remarkable change had taken place in the experience of these same disciples. They were now convinced that it was not a lost cause. The man who had died on the cross was one whose life had met with divine approval. He had not died because of his own sins but like the suffering servant of the prophet Isaiah he had died for the sake of others. They were sure now that he was the true Messiah, the nature of whose mission they had not understood before his crucifixion. His death on the cross did not mean the end of the cause for which he stood. In fact that cause was now more alive than it had ever been before. The kingdom would yet be established. His return to earth to complete the program already begun would be accomplished in the near future. With these convictions in the minds of the disciples the Christian movement was inaugurated and it was this movement that produced the writings in our New Testament.

SUMMARIES AND COMMENTARIES
THE PAULINE LETTERS

Approximately one third of the New Testament consists of letters written by the Apostle Paul and addressed to the Christian churches of his day. Since these letters are older than any of the Gospel accounts of the life of Jesus they constitute the most reliable source that we have today for information concerning the early history of the Christian movement. With few exceptions these letters were written in response to conditions which existed in the particular churches with which Paul had been associated. It was not until some time after his death that these letters were circulated among the churches and read along with the Old Testament scriptures as a part of the regular services of worship. It was still later that they came to be regarded as inspired writings comparable to the sacred scriptures of Judaism.

To understand the contents of these letters it is necessary to know something about the man who wrote them as well as the particular circumstances under which they were written. Fortunately for us considerable information along this line is available within the letters themselves. This information can be supplemented by the biographical accounts which were written by Luke and included in the book of Acts. Luke had been a companion of Paul and therefore had first hand information even though we may safely assume that in some instances he was somewhat biased in what he had to say.

Paul was a native of Tarsus, a city of considerable importance in the Graeco-Roman world. He was a descendant of the Hebrew tribe of Benjamin and was named Saul after Israel's first king. Being raised in a Jewish home he was taught the Old Testament scriptures and brought up in strict accordance with the beliefs and practices of the Pharisee sect. As he grew older he was sent to the city of Jerusalem where he studied under Gamaliel one of the leading Jewish rabbis of that day. Later he returned to Tarsus and while we have no direct information on this point, it can be assumed that he attended the Greek university which was located in that city. A crucial turning point in his career came after he returned to Jerusalem and began studies in preparation for becoming a rabbi. As a devoted and loyal Jew of the Pharisee sect his attention was given primarily to a detailed analysis of the requirements set forth in the Mosaic law. He became familiar not only with the law itself but with the explanations and commentaries made by the leading rabbis of the Jewish faith. In harmony with one of the basic doctrines of Judaism he believed that salvation could be obtained only by obedience to all of the laws which God had given to his people. But as Paul pursued his studies he became conscious of the fact that a mere knowledge concerning what one ought to do did not produce the desire to do it. Furthermore, he realized that it is one's desires that give rise to his actions and the law is unable to give one the desires that are necessary to meet its requirements. In fact the situation was even worse than that, for the knowledge that one ought not to do certain things would often act as a stimulus creating the desire to do it. This conflict between duty and desire became for Paul an intolerable situation and because of it he gave up his plans for becoming a rabbi. To compensate for his failure to carry out his original plans he was anxious to find something of real merit that he might do. This he believed he had found in the need for suppressing a new religious movement which he regarded as both dangerous and heretical.

This movement was being promulgated by a group of people who claimed to be followers of Jesus, a man who had been crucified but whom they now believed had risen from the dead, ascended to heaven, and would return to earth in power and great glory. To put an end to this movement was something to which Paul now devoted himself with the utmost zeal. He hunted down the members of this group, had them committed to prison, and threatened with death. But as he did so he could not help but be impressed by the way in which the Christians met the persecutions inflicted upon them. The stoning of Stephen was one of these incidents. With perfect calm and an inner peace of mind he knelt down and prayed that those who were casting the stones might be forgiven. It was perfectly evident that these Christians possessed that which Paul desired more than anything else. They had the peace of mind that comes with a clear conscience and a deep conviction that they are living in harmony with the will of God. Paul came to realize that there must be some connection between the faith in Jesus which these persons possessed and manner of living which they exhibited. No doubt this conviction was growing upon him for some time but the climactic turning point in his career came while he was on the road to Damascus. Convinced now that Jesus was a righteous man and that his death on the cross was not the just punishment of a criminal but rather that of a martyr who died for a noble cause, he was ready to give himself to that same cause. The cause had not perished with the death on a cross of the one who had espoused it. In fact it was now more alive than it had been before and it pointed the way to a salvation that could not be achieved by obedience to a set of laws that were contrary to human desires.

Paul's decision to cast his lot with the members of the Christian community did not make him a missionary all at once. It was about fourteen years before his work as a leader in the new movement received any general recognition. During this time he had ample opportunity to rethink his religious conceptions, systematize his understanding of the meaning of Jesus' career on earth, and formulate plans for spreading a knowledge of the Gospel throughout the Graeco-Roman world. Eventually he was invited by Barnabas to come to the church at Antioch and assist in the work being done in that place. After serving this church for a brief period he began a series of missionary journeys in order that the new Gospel might be carried to the various cities and villages of the then known world. It was while engaged in these missionary activities that he wrote the letters which have been preserved in the New Testament.

THE LETTER TO THE GALATIANS

Summary

The occasion for this letter was a controversy which had developed among the churches in Galatia, especially the one in Antioch, concerning the matter of requiring the Gentile Christians to obey the Mosaic laws. One of these laws in particular was very much in question. It had to do with circumcision, a religious rite which had meant for the Jews much the same thing as baptism came to mean for the Christians of a later period. The Christians whose background had been in Judaism could see no reason why this rite should not be required of all Christians the same as it had been for the Jews. As they understood it the laws given by God through Moses were binding for all time and could never be set aside by human beings, nor by any set of circumstances that might arise. When those of a Gentile background became followers of Jesus and sought admission to the Christian churches they could see no particular value in the observance of this rite and would like to be excused from it. Paul, who had been invited to work with the Gentile element in the church, was sympathetic with their position. The experiences which he had encountered with the law prior to his conversion had convinced him that no one could ever be saved by mere obedience to a set of external laws. His own conversion to the Christian faith had been brought about by the conviction that it was the spirit that had been manifest in the life of Jesus taking possession of the hearts and minds of individuals which enabled them to be saved. Accordingly, if Gentile Christians were possessed by this spirit, which for Paul was the true meaning of faith, it made little or no difference at all whether they conformed to the letter of the Mosaic laws. So long as Paul remained with these churches the Jewish and Gentile elements seemed to get along without any serious trouble, each group following the dictates of their individual consciences. But after Paul left for one of his missionary tours, prominent officials of the church in Jerusalem came down to visit the newly established churches in Galatia and then the trouble began.

These visitors insisted that the law concerning circumcision as well as the other requirements of the Mosaic law were binding on all Christians including those coming from a Gentile background. Furthermore, they launched a vicious attack on Paul personally because of the attitude he had taken on this matter. They even went so far as to charge that he was an imposter and was guilty of misleading the membership of the church. It was in response to these charges that Paul wrote this letter.

At the beginning of the letter he expressed astonishment at what had taken place during his absence from them. He was surprised at the attitude taken by the so-called leaders of the church at Jerusalem and he was deeply disappointed when the people among whom he had labored had been persuaded by these visiting brethren to turn from the message which he had proclaimed and accept as obligatory the requirements which had been characteristic of Jewish legalism. Replying to the accusation that he was not a qualified leader of the Christian community, Paul defended his apostleship by declaring that it was God rather than men who had called him to that office. In support of this claim he reviewed the experiences which had led to his conversion and the circumstances under which he had carried on his work among the churches. He described his relationship to the so-called "pillars of the church" at Jerusalem explaining both the purpose and the outcome of his conferences with them. He stated that while he had not received from them any directive concerning the content of the message he was to proclaim, they were fully informed about the work he was doing and had given their approval to it specifying in particular that he should devote his main efforts toward working with those who were entering the church from a Gentile background.

Following this introduction Paul proceeds to the main point of the letter which was to explain and to clarify his position concerning the law. This he did by pointing out both its uses and its limitations as a means of obtaining salvation. The law is useful, he maintained, to point out the defects in one's character. In this respect its function is like that of a looking-glass which reveals blemishes but does not remove them. Again, he says, "the law is the custodian to bring one to faith in Christ" and when this goal has been reached the law is no longer necessary. "No man is justified before God by the law." It is only by faith in Christ that men are justified. By faith Paul means something more than a mere intellectual assent to a number of facts in connection with the life of Jesus. He means a commitment on the part of the individual to the way of life which was exemplified in the person of Jesus. One who is possessed by the same spirit that was present in him will be saved from sin and the spiritual death which it brings. He will be saved because his desires and his whole nature will be so transformed that he will do what is right because he wants to act that way rather than because he thinks it is a duty to be performed in order to obtain a reward.

Having stated his position in regard to the law Paul presents a series of arguments in support of it. For example, he refers to Abraham as the father of the faithful and insists that his righteousness could not have been obtained by obedience to the Mosaic laws because those laws were not given until centuries after Abraham had died. Hence, it must be that he obtained it by faith. But if Abraham's righteousness was by faith the same must be true for all of his spiritual descendants. When God made his great promise to Abraham all of his descendants were included. Christians are, according to Paul, of the seed of Abraham for it is said "if you are Christ's you are Abraham's seed and heirs according to the promise." The same point is elaborated somewhat further in the allegory of Abraham's two sons. One of these, Ishmael, was born of the slave woman but the other son, Isaac, was born of a free woman. Ishmael represents those who are under bondage to the law while Isaac represents those who are free in Christ. "For freedom Christ has set us free; stand fast therefore, and do not submit again to a yoke of slavery."

The letter concludes with a description of the kind of life that one will live when he is filled with the spirit of God. It stands in sharp contrast with the kind of life that pursues the desires of the flesh. It is the quality of living that determines whether one is possessed by the spirit of Christ.

Commentary

The letter to the Galatians is important for several reasons. First of all, it is among the earliest if not the earliest of all the writings in the New Testament. Secondly, it gives us an insight into the problems which arose in the Christian churches of the first century. Thirdly, and most important of all, is the fact that it reveals one of the most essential elements in Paul's conception of Christianity. The letter has sometimes been called "Paul's declaration of independence". This designation means freedom from bondage to laws of any kind whether they are human laws or divine laws. It was on this particular point that Paul made a definite break not only with Judaism but with those Christians of Jewish descent who thought of the new religion in terms of obedience both to the laws given by Moses and also the ones enunciated by Jesus.

These two conceptions of Christianity were in general held respectively by the Jewish and the Gentile elements in the membership of the Christian church. Those with a Jewish background held what may be called a "legalistic" conception of religion while the Gentile element under the leadership of Paul believed in a "mystical" conception. According to the latter view, salvation can never be achieved by trying to obey the requirements of the law. The reason is that human nature is so constituted that one necessarily follows the desires of his own heart and so long as these desires are contrary to the requirements of the law the result will be disobedience and a sense of guilt. When Paul speaks of salvation by faith he means that situation in which the desires have been changed so that what one wants to do will coincide with what he ought to do. This type of transformation is something that man cannot bring about by himself alone. It can take place only when the spirit of God which was in Christ takes possession of one's heart and mind. This is the very essence of Christian mysticism. It means a union or "oneness" of the individual and God. In other words God dwells within the life of the individual and his nature is changed thereby from one that is prone to do evil to one that is prone to do what is good. This, for Paul, was the real meaning of salvation. The career of Jesus on this earth was significant because it illustrated what can happen to any human being who allows the spirit of God to take full possession of him. This idea is clearly expressed in the words of Paul when he says "I live, yet not I; it is Christ who lives and abides in me."

Paul's argument was not, however, convincing to all the members of the Christian community. Many of them, especially those of a Jewish background and understanding, still held to the legalistic view. The conflict between the legalistic and the mystical interpretations of religion can be traced through all the successive periods of Christian history. It is still one of the vital issues in contemporary theology.

THE THESSALONIAN LETTERS

Summary

Two letters which Paul wrote to the church in Thessalonica have been preserved in the New Testament. The first letter was written to a community of believers who had been Christians for only a short period of time, probably no more than a few months. We learn from the book of Acts that during Paul's stay in the city of Thessalonica he preached in a Jewish synagogue on three successive Sabbath days. He evidently stayed in the city for some time after this and carried on his work among the Gentiles. His ministry was successful at least to the extent that he won converts to Christianity from both groups. He did, however, encounter opposition especially from the Jews who resented very much the fact that he was able to win followers from their numbers. Because of their opposition Paul felt that it was wise to leave the city lest the newly formed Christian community would be persecuted as he had been. He regretted that he must leave them before they were well established in the faith and it was his hope that he might visit them again in the near future. When sickness prevented him from doing this he sent his colleague Timothy to strengthen the group and report to him on the progress that had been made. When Timothy returned with the good news that the members of the church were standing firm in their new faith Paul wrote this letter.

He congratulates them on their fidelity to the Gospel which he had proclaimed while among them and urges them to remain steadfast in the faith. Knowing something about the temptations to evil conduct which were present in that pagan city he warned them against sensuality and various forms of self-seeking which were contrary to the spirit of the Christian way of life. But the main purpose of this letter was to deal with a special problem which had developed since the time when Paul had left the city. It seems that Paul had shared with the believers at Thessalonica his belief that the end of the age would come in the very near future. This belief was in part an inheritance from Jewish apocalypticism. It was held that the messianic kingdom would be ushered in by a sudden catastrophic event at which time the heavenly messiah would descend on the clouds from heaven with power and great glory. When the first Christians accepted the idea that the man who had died on the cross was the real Messiah, they were convinced that he must return to earth to complete the work which he had begun. The manner of his second coming was conceived in accordance with the apocalyptic conceptions. This belief was common among the early Christians, and Paul accepted it along with the rest. Although the Christians were quite insistent that no one knew the exact time when this second coming would take place, they felt sure that it would occur during the lifetime of those who were then members of the Christian community.

After Paul left Thessalonica some of the people who belonged to the church had died. Since Jesus had not returned some serious doubts had arisen in the minds of those who were still living. They had been led to believe that Jesus would return before any of their number had died. As they saw it, Paul had been mistaken on this point and that caused them to wonder whether he might not have been mistaken on other points as well. Obviously, an explanation of some kind was in order and it was this situation more than any other single factor that prompted the writing of this letter.

Paul's statement in regard to this matter was to the effect that he had in no way abandoned his faith that the return of Jesus to this earth would take place in the near future. Concerning those who had died or who might die before Jesus returned he said that they would be raised from the dead and would share equally with those who were still living at that time. "For our Lord himself shall descend from heaven, with a shout and the voice of the archangel and the trumpet of God, and the dead in Christ shall rise first." To this statement he then adds "then we who are alive and remain shall be caught up together with them to meet our Lord in the air, and so shall we ever be with the Lord." The letter closes with a reminder that the day of the Lord will come as a thief in the night. No one knows just when it will come but all are admonished to live in such a way that they will be ready for it at any moment.

The second letter to the Thessalonians is in one sense a follow up of the first letter. Evidently, the first letter had been well received. The people were satisfied with his explanation concerning those who had died and they were ready and willing to suffer persecution if need be in order to remain true to the Gospel which Paul had preached. But on one point some of the members of the Christian community were overly zealous. They took Paul's teaching about the nearness of the end of the age so seriously that they stopped making any plans for the future. Indeed some of them stopped doing any work at all believing that in this way they were demonstrating their faith in the nearness of the great event. Those who did not work were of course a burden to those who did work and this situation constituted a new problem. Paul had something to say concerning it.

After commending the group for their loyalty and assuring them that God will deal justly with their persecutors, he proceeds to the main point of the letter. Although the coming of the day of the Lord is near, it is not as close as some of them think it is. Actually, a report had been circulated among them to the effect that the day had already come. Paul tells them not to be deceived on this matter for that day will not come until after certain events have taken place and these have not occurred yet. The specific events to which he refers have to do with the coming of an Anti-Christ, someone in whom the power of Satan has become incarnate and who will establish himself in the Temple at Jerusalem working with signs and wonders to deceive the people. The basis for Paul's statement along this line is found in the Jewish apocalyptic writings which were fairly well known at that time. Concerning the coming of this lawless one, Paul says that his activities are already in operation. They would be carried out more fully except for the fact that he is now being restrained. Presumably Paul meant that it was the Roman government that was holding him back. In due time he will be revealed "and the Lord Jesus will slay him with the breath of his mouth and destroy him with the brightness of his coming." The letter closes with admonition to continue with their regular lines of work and not to wait in idleness for the return of Jesus.

Commentary

The two letters to the Thessalonians are of interest from an historical point of view because they reveal conditions which existed in the newly formed Christian communities. They are also of value in that they indicate something of the extent to which the early church was influenced by Jewish apocalypticism in its beliefs concerning the second coming of Christ and the setting up of the messianic kingdom. Jewish apocalypses had taught that there would be a resurrection of the dead in connection with the other events which would usher in the new age. Paul was able to make use of these apocalyptic conceptions in answering the questions which had so troubled the Christians in Thessalonica.

Both of these letters were addressed to this one church and they were occasioned by the problems associated with that particular group of persons. It is quite unlikely that Paul anticipated any further use to be made of them. There is little if anything in them that throws much light on the theological issues involved in Paul's interpretation of Christianity. They do however indicate the type of instruction which he gave to the newcomers in the Christian movement.

THE LETTERS TO THE CORINTHIANS

Summary

Paul wrote at least four different letters to the church at Corinth. Three of these have been included in the New Testament. In what is now called I Corinthians there is a reference to a former letter in which instruction had been given concerning the type of conduct which should not be tolerated in a Christian church. II Corinthians as it now stands is made up of two different letters. Chapters 10-13 belong to what is often referred to as the "painful letter" in which Paul replies to the many false charges that have been made concerning him and his work. Chapters 1-9 are written in a different and conciliatory tone which would seem to indicate that it was written after the painful letter had been received and accepted by the members of the church. The largest part of Paul's correspondence was with the church at Corinth for the problems encountered in this place were more numerous than he had found in other cities and if the Gospel could be successful here there was good reason for believing it could have results that would be equally as good in any other place.

Corinth was an important city in Paul's day. It was a center for Greek culture and it was a busy commercial city with a cosmopolitan atmosphere that brought together people and customs from different parts of the world. It was generally known as a city that was devoted to pleasure seeking. Pagan religions with their sexual rites and ceremonies were in evidence and both materialism and immorality were the accepted order of the day. In view of these conditions it is no wonder Paul said he began his Corinthian mission with "fear and trembling." His work was, however, successful from the beginning. He was especially anxious to guide these new converts with reference to the many perplexing problems that were bound to arise. In other places it was the Jewish element with its legalistic tendencies that created difficulties but in Corinth it was the moral problem

that caused the greater anxiety. The church had drawn into its membership people from many different quarters, including those whose training
and environment were foreign to the Hebrew standards of morality. Paul
was deeply concerned that the Christian church in Corinth should make
no compromise with the morality that was customary in a pagan society.

The longest of the letters written to this church is the one known in
our New Testament as I Corinthians. It contains 16 chapters and has to
do with a wide variety of topics. The first one mentioned is that of divisions or parties within the church. Four distinct factions are listed
corresponding with the four individuals whose teachings were followed
by the respective groups. The four teachers were Paul, Apollos, Cephas,
and Christ. It had been reported to Paul by the household of Chloe that
serious quarrels had taken place among these factions. Evidently the
spirit of independent thinking emphasized so strongly by the Greeks was
having its influence among the Christians in Corinth. Paul's manner of
dealing with the problem is noteworthy. He does not insist that all the
members of the community shall think alike on every subject, nor does
he advocate that someone with authority shall tell the others what to
believe. What he does insist upon is a unity of spirit and of purpose which
will allow each group to learn from the others. The kind of unity that he
recommends for the church is similar to that which unifies a group of
scientists who are working independently toward a more adequate understanding of a group of problems.

On the subject of immorality within the membership of the church
Paul is very explicit. This type of conduct must not be tolerated among
the believers. If any of their number persists in following the low standards of the pagans they should be excluded from membership. Association
with evil doers cannot be avoided so long as they are living in a wicked
city, but it need not be permitted within the group that is called Christian.
It is the function of the church to set a high standard for the society in
which it exists and this cannot be done by permitting low standards among
their own members. "Do you not know that a little leaven ferments the
whole lump of dough? Cleanse out the old leaven, that you may be fresh
dough, as you really are unleavened."

When disputes arise among members of the Christian community
they should be settled peaceably without going to a civil court. "To have
lawsuits at all with one another is defeat for you. Why not rather suffer
wrong?" Paul refers to a popular Jewish belief that the saints are to have
a part in the judgment of the world. Certainly they are not qualified to do
this if they are unable to settle difficulties among themselves.

Sex morality was a real problem in the church at Corinth. Neither monogamy nor chastity was regarded as obligatory in the pagan society where many of the church members had been reared before becoming Christians. Paul's instruction in regard to marriage must be considered in the light of his belief concerning the imminence of the second coming of Christ as well as his desire to have the church at Corinth exemplify a high standard of living in this respect. The same can be said about his advice concerning the impropriety of women speaking in church. In the city of Corinth it was customary for the temple prostitutes to speak in public and to protect the reputation of the women in the Christian church he thought it would be wise for them to remain silent. He explains, however, that this is merely his personal opinion for he has received no direct revelation to this effect.

In regard to the eating of meat that has been obtained from animals that were sacrificed to idols the instruction given is to the effect that everyone should follow the dictates of his own conscience, the only condition being that each person should have respect for the conscience of the person who does not agree with him. One should refrain from needlessly offending the other person even though by so doing it is necessary for him to curb his own appetite. It was customary in all of the Christian churches to commemorate the events associated with Jesus' death and resurrection by partaking of a common meal together. Some of the people at Corinth had failed to see the significance of this meal and had made of it an occasion for feasting. Paul explains that the purpose of this meal is not for the enjoyment of eating and drinking together but rather for a renewed dedication to the spirit which was made manifest in the life and death of Jesus. In other words it was a time when each individual should examine his own heart and life and bring them into harmony with the spirit that was in Christ. Any grievances which they have with one another should be put away in preparation for the eating of the meal together.

Spiritual gifts among the various members of the church is another topic which is treated at some length in this letter. Using the analogy of the human body in which each organ has its special function to perform and no one of them can be regarded as more vital than another, the same principle applies within the church which is the body of Christ. Some of the members have the gift of prophecy, others that of teaching, and there are those whose special gift is that of offering help in carrying forward the work of the church. Those who are apostles, or prophets, are not to think of themselves as superior to those who exercise other gifts for all of these are necessary and the church would not be complete if any of them were missing. To those who boasted that they had the gift of tongues and were therefore in a position to exercise lordship over others, Paul writes that this particular gift like all of the others should be evaluated in terms of its usefulness in promoting the Christian way of life. He did not condemn this gift for those who might find it useful but he did say that so far as he was concerned it was better to speak a few words that would be understood by others than it would be to speak at great length in an unknown tongue that is quite unintelligible to those who might hear it.

Following the discussion of spiritual gifts is Paul's immortal hymn to Christian love. This is one of the great classics of Christian literature. It makes the motive of love the foundation for all Christian conduct. What wisdom was for the Greeks is what love is for the Christian. "And now abideth three things, faith, hope, and love, but the greatest of these is love."

After the discourse on love Paul writes about the resurrection. For him the subject is of primary importance for he considers it the basis upon which the whole structure of Christianity rests. If Christ is not risen, he says, then our hope is in vain. The fact of Christ's resurrection is attested by a large number of witnesses of whom Paul counts himself one of the last. The significance of the resurrection is something more than a vindication of the Messiahship of Jesus. It is an assurance that what happened in the case of Jesus can and will happen again to all those who believe in him. The resurrection of the righteous will be associated with the second coming of Christ. "Then this corruptible will put on incorruption, and this mortal will put on immortality. Then shall be brought to pass the saying that is written 'Death shall be swallowed up in victory.'" The letter closes with an appeal for a contribution to help provide for the poor among the Christians in Jerusalem. He will stop at Corinth on his way to Jerusalem and take their gift with him.

The so-called "painful letter" which is found in the last four chapters of our *II Corinthians* contains Paul's defense of himself and the work he has been doing. It was his reply to the charges made against him by his enemies including the Jewish legalists. They had said that he was an imposter who had not been authorized by the proper authorities to work among the churches. They supported their charge by pointing out that he had a "thorn in the flesh" which meant some physical defect that according to ancient Jewish regulations would have barred one from the priesthood. They maintained, further, that he had supported himself by doing manual labor rather than accept entertainment from the members of the church. This, in their judgment, was an admission on his part that he was not qualified to be supported in the way that was customary for duly authorized missionaries. Again, they accused Paul of cowardice on the grounds that he was bold so long as he was writing letters but he was very mild when present with them in person. Other charges of a similar nature were made in an all-out attempt to discredit the work he had been doing with them.

To all of these charges Paul makes a vigorous reply. He shows wherein the charges are false and he recounts for the people at Corinth the many trials and hardships which he has suffered for their sake and for the sake of the Gospel. Although he apologizes for seeming to boast of his own attainments, he explains the necessity for doing it. He indicates further that his greatest disappointment lies not in the fact that charges of this sort have been made about him but rather that the members of the Corinthian church have apparently been persuaded by them.

The first nine chapters of what is now called *II Corinthians* is a letter which appears to have been written some time after the painful letter has been received and accepted by the church. This letter contains an expression of gratitude for the change that has taken place among the believers at Corinth. Paul rejoices that they are now on the right track again and he summarizes for them the essential meaning of the Gospel which he proclaimed to them at first. Using the language of the Old Testament prophet Jeremiah he tells them that the Christian Gospel is none other than the new covenant which has been written "not on tablets of stone but on the fleshy tablets of the human heart." Toward the close of the letter he reminds them again of the collection to be taken for the poor in Jerusalem.

Commentary

Although all of the Corinthian letters were addressed to a single church and were concerned primarily with local problems existing at that time, they are nevertheless of special interest to the student of the New Testament. One of the reasons for this is the fact that they were written at an early date. They therefore are able to throw considerable light on the character of the Christian movement prior to the writing of any of the Gospel accounts of the life of Jesus. Paul's statements concerning the resurrection of Jesus constitute the earliest record of that event that has been preserved. The same is true of his account of the institution of the Lord's supper. His remarks concerning the gift of tongues along with the other gifts of the spirit helps us to understand the way in which these manifestations were viewed by the early church. Finally, the many problems discussed in our I Corinthians tell us a great deal about the conditions which prevailed at that time.

Paul's account of the resurrection enables us to see how his view differed from that of the ancient Greeks and also from the one found in certain portions of the Old Testament. The Greeks like many of the Orientals believed in the doctrine of the immortality of the soul. According to this view souls have neither a beginning nor an end. They are eternal realities which are capable of existing apart from the body in which they may have been incarnated. This was contrary to the Hebrew conception which viewed man as a single unit including body, soul, and spirit. Hence the soul was not something which existed apart from the body. After death all went down to Sheol, a cavern below the earth, but there was no memory or consciousness of any kind that attended this state of existence. In contrast with these views Paul believed in a genuine resurrection from the dead in which one's individuality and moral worth would be preserved. But it was not to be a reanimation of the corpse and a continuation of life as it had been before. Flesh and blood, he tells us, will not inherit the kingdom. The body that is raised will not be the natural body but rather a spiritual body. He does not tell us what this spiritual body will be like but he is sure that it will be a body of some kind for the personality includes body, soul, and spirit, and salvation has not been achieved until all three have been transformed together. The Gnostics of Paul's day believing that only spirit is good and all matter is evil had taught that Jesus did not possess a physical body but had only appeared to do so. For Paul this position was untenable for unless Jesus possessed a body in common with other human beings his triumph over evil would have no significance for them. The resurrection of Jesus meant a triumph of the entire personality over the forces of evil and what it meant for him it means also for all those who put their trust in him. It was this conception which led the Christians of a later day to include in their formulation of the creed the words "I believe in the resurrection of the body and the life everlasting."

THE LETTER TO THE ROMANS

Summary

Paul had promised the church at Corinth that he would visit them again as soon as he had the opportunity. It was not long after sending his last letter to them that the opportunity came and he was able to spend several months with them. It was during this time, probably the latter part of the year 57 A.D. that he wrote the letter to the church at Rome. It was the most ambitious of all his letters and the only one in which he presented a systematic account of his understanding of the Gospel. Since he had not visited the church at Rome and was unfamiliar with their local problems the letter was not written in the form which had been used in his earlier correspondence with the other churches. Instead it was a carefully prepared statement of what he regarded as the essential elements of the Christian religion. He wanted the Gospel to be proclaimed throughout the then known world and it seemed most appropriate that he should not only visit the church at Rome but gain its full support for the missionary program which he had in mind. We do not know how the church at Rome was started but it was a going concern in Paul's day and there were good reasons for believing that it would soon become one of the leading Christian churches of the world. Paul wanted them to have a firsthand knowledge of the Gospel which he preached and being unable to visit them in person during the immediate future he set forth his convictions in a letter addressed to them.

There are sixteen chapters in the letter and parts of these are so closely written that a full explanation of his meaning would require a large volume of commentary. The main substance of the letter can be summarized briefly by stating the answers given to a number of pertinent questions. These questions include such items as the following. What is the Gospel? Who needs it? Why is it needed? What is the nature of salvation? How is it achieved? What difference does it make in the life of the individual? What difference does it make with reference to society as a whole? There are to be sure many other points discussed in the letter but these are sufficient to indicate its general character.

The Gospel, we are told, is the power of God unto salvation. "For in it the righteousness of God is revealed through faith." Man is a sinful creature. He follows the desires of his own heart and he is powerless to change these desires by himself alone. It is only through the power of God working in cooperation with the human spirit that these desires can be changed and brought into harmony with the divine will. The life of Jesus is an illustration of the way in which the power of God can work in and through a human life, thus enabling it to overcome the temptations to evil which are ever-present in the world in which one lives. The same power that enabled Jesus to overcome temptations is also available to all those who have faith in him. The faith by which the righteousness of God is revealed involves beliefs but it also includes something more than these. It is something that grips the entire personality and finds expression not only in what one thinks but in his feelings, attitudes, and actions as well. The salvation of which Paul writes is salvation from the power of evil which entices man to sin against himself as well as against God. In other words it is salvation from sin rather than being spared the hardships and difficulties that are characteristic of finite existence. It means a transformation of one's nature so that what one wants to do will coincide with what he ought to do.

This salvation is needed by everyone, for all have sinned and come short of the glory of God. It is just as necessary for the Jew as it is for the Gentile. It is necessary even for those who feel that they do not need it. In fact, they may be the ones who are most in need of it. How well one thinks of himself is determined by the standard which he uses in judging himself. Anyone who measures himself by the righteousness of God will know that he falls short and is in need of improvement. The salvation of which Paul speaks is not something that will automatically and all at once make a person's character equal to the righteousness of God. But it will move him in that direction and keep bringing him ever nearer to that goal. But, again, it is important to know that this salvation is available only to those who recognize their need for it and who are receptive to the divine power which is constantly being offered to them.

In his discussion of the way in which salvation is to be achieved Paul presents again the same arguments which he used in the letter to the Galatians. He places emphasis on the fact that it is not brought about by efforts on the part of the individual to observe the requirements of the law. It makes no difference so far as this point is concerned whether the laws are human or divine in their origin. Laws of any kind are powerless to make people good. Evidence of this can be seen in the state of society as it existed in Rome at that time. The Romans had for a long time boasted of the superior quality of their system of laws. It was true that their laws were among the best the nations of the world had known up to that time. But in spite of these laws Roman society had become notoriously corrupt. The state of this corruption is indicated in the closing verses of the first chapter of the letter. The Jews, Paul argues, are in this respect no better off than the Romans. The Romans have had their human laws and the Jews have had divine laws but in neither case have the laws changed the desires of men or transformed their natures from that which is evil into that which is good. It is only by faith that a transformation of this kind can take place. It is in this connection that Paul writes about justification by faith. Having pointed out that "no human being can be justified in the sight of God for having kept the law; law brings only consciousness of sin" he goes on to say "and all are justified by God's free grace alone, through his act of liberation in the person of Jesus Christ." And again, he says, "For our argument is that a man is justified by faith quite apart from success in keeping the law." Men are in need of justification because they are estranged from God. They are not living in harmony with their own best interests and this is equivalent to saying they are not in harmony with the divine will. Justification is that which overcomes the estrangement and puts them on the right track. This happens when the spirit of God takes possession of one's heart and life. It is then that his desires are changed and he becomes "a new creature." This is what Paul means by salvation.

Having developed his argument concerning the means of salvation Paul illustrates his position by referring to Abraham as he did in the letter to the Galatians. It was Abraham's faith that was "counted to him as righteousness" and it is by faith that those who are his spiritual descendants can be saved. Jesus is the supreme example of faith in that he was a human being in whom the spirit of God was manifested more completely than in any other person. In this respect Paul thinks of him as the typical or ideal man in the same way that Adam was regarded as the type or symbol of the human race. Just as in Adam we all died, so in Christ are we all made alive. Adam's disobedience illustrates what happens in the lives of all human beings, and Jesus' triumph over the forces of evil illustrates what can happen when the spirit that was present in him takes possession of one's entire nature. This point, Paul insists, is the true meaning of Christian baptism. It symbolizes the death and burial of one's sinful nature and a resurrection into a new quality of living. Paul's own experience with the law when he was studying to become a rabbi is described at some length to illustrate again the impotence of the law in contrast with the power of faith to transform one's nature. Trying to achieve salvation through obedience to the law was indeed a miserable type of existence. It was comparable to having a dead person strapped to one's own body. In this state of affairs one is a slave to sin. "I do not even acknowledge my own actions as mine, for what I do is not what I want to do, but what I detest." And again, "if what I do is against my will, clearly it is no longer I who am the agent, but sin that has its lodging in me." It is under these conditions that one cries out "O wretched man that I am, who can deliver me from this body of sin and of death?" The answer is that deliverance comes through faith in Jesus Christ. "There is now no condemnation for those who are united with Christ Jesus, because in Christ Jesus the life-giving law of the spirit has set you free from the law of sin and death."

The effects of salvation will be manifest first of all in the changed life of the individual. As this takes place in increasing numbers it will mean the transformation of society as well. The life of the spirit which frees one from bondage to the law does not give one the license to sin nor does it mean that laws can legitimately be violated just because they conflict with one's immediate desires. The Christian will be a law-abiding citizen but his freedom will consist in the fact that he no longer wants to act contrary to them. He will do what is right because he desires to act that way rather than doing it from a pure sense of duty or as a means of gaining a reward.

With reference to the future of the Jewish people Paul expresses the hope that they too will be included with the ones who are saved through the Gospel. Since the Gospel was of divine origin and it was through faith that the great heroes of Israel achieved righteousness, it seems strange that the Jews would have rejected it. When they refused to accept it the opportunity was extended to the Gentiles. But Paul does not envisage a complete break between Judaism and Christianity. It is his belief that the Jews will in time come to see the light and accept it since God is not willing that any should perish but that all might be saved.

The closing part of the letter contains instruction in the manner of living. He tells the Christians at Rome to have respect for the civil government for "the powers that be are ordained of God." He does not mean by this that the Christian should obey the civil laws when they are in conflict with the laws of God but rather that he should not attempt to hide his conduct from the rulers nor escape the punishment which the state inflicts. Earthly governments are not perfect and some of their laws are bound to be unjust. Nevertheless, they do preserve order in society and it is only proper and right that the Christian should support them. As in the other letters to different churches he asks the Christians at Rome to contribute to the fund which he is gathering for the relief of the poor in Jerusalem.

Commentary

In no portion of the New Testament is the dynamic and universal character of Christianity set forth more clearly than in Paul's letter to the Romans. Evidence of this can be seen in the fact that so many of the revival and reform movements in the course of Christian history have been started and promulgated by a restudy of this portion of the New Testament. In the 16th century Martin Luther's commentary on Romans was an important factor in the promotion of the Protestant reformation, and again in the 20th century when Karl Barth published his analysis of Romans, a new era was introduced in the contemporary interpretations of Christianity. Paul's letter to the church in Rome is without question one of the great documents in Christian literature. It has furnished the inspiration and guidance for many of the important developments that have taken place in the life of the church during the past and in all likelihood it will continue to do so in the future.

The dynamic character of the Gospel as Paul understands it can be seen in the introductory portions of the letter for it is there that he refers to it as something that is powerful. It is, he tells us, "the power of God unto salvation." The Gospel is something more than the acceptance of a set of speculative ideas, even though these are not necessarily excluded. It is none other than the righteousness of God which is an active force operating in the lives of people who are ready and willing to receive it. It is available to all those who recognize their need for it regardless of their race or religious background. It does for those persons who are willing to accept it something which they are wholly unable to do all by themselves. It produces within them a changed nature so that the desires of their hearts will coincide with what they ought to do.

The universality of the Gospel is exemplified in the way in which it completely transcends all distinctions between Jew and Gentile. This is an important item for among the early Christians as well as in other communities there were those who held that salvation was only for the Jews. Paul is addressing this letter to a church whose membership is composed of people from both Jewish and Gentile backgrounds and he wants to set forth the meaning of the Gospel in terms that will be intelligible to all of them. Because he is familiar with both Judaism and Hellenistic culture he is able to use concepts drawn from each of these sources to communicate his version of Christianity. Thus we find him using the terminology of Jewish eschatology and apocalypticism as well as the language of the mystery cults and other forms of Gentile religion in explaining his conception of the real significance of the life, death, and resurrection of Jesus. This use of terms drawn from such different sources was not without its dangers for his readers might very well interpret these terms in a manner that was other than he intended. He did not want to convey the idea that the use of these terms in connection with the Christian religion was exactly like what either the Jews or the Gentiles had been taught. He used them rather for the purpose of pointing out similarities which would be an aid toward their proper understanding.

Salvation, as this term had been used by the Jews of Paul's day referred primarily to a future event when the kingdoms of this earth would be brought to an end and the new age identified as the kingdom of God would be established. The saved would be those who were not destroyed at that time but who would be permitted to live under the new order of things. While Paul does not reject this view entirely he couples with it the idea that salvation is something to be achieved here and now as well as in the future. It means being saved from yielding to the evil temptations that are met in our daily life. This is achieved not by conformity to duty in obedience to laws but by faith in the righteousness of God which was manifested in the life of Jesus the Christ. In support of this conviction Paul quotes from the Old Testament prophet Habakkuk the words, "the just man shall live by his faith." Paul's use of the word "faith" is somewhat different from that of the ancient prophet for Habakkuk was speaking about our belief concerning the future that was in store for those who lived in obedience to the commands of God while Paul is talking about a salvation that is "apart from the law." Thus we see how he used a familiar Hebrew term to communicate to his readers a concept that was in some respects new to them.

In his discussion of the need for salvation Paul implies what has often been called the doctrine of original sin. The Adam of the Genesis story is interpreted as a reference to all mankind. The same tendency toward evil that was present in him is also present in every human being. Yielding to these temptations is what brings about an estrangement between the individual and God. To explain the way in which this estrangement can be overcome Paul draws analogies from customary court procedures and from concepts used in the mystery cults. He shows how all men are guilty before God and in this connection he speaks of justification and redemption. When the sinner acknowledges his guilt he is accepted by God, and past sins are no longer held against him. He is justified in the sense that the estrangement has been overcome and he is now in accord with the divine will. This does not mean that he will never sin again but it does mean that he will continually be aware of his need for improvement and will ever seek divine aid for its accomplishment. To explain the change that takes place in one's life when he has experienced justification and has been possessed by the same Spirit that was present in Jesus, Paul uses the language of the mystery cults. Just as the heroic redeemer of these cults experienced a death, burial, and resurrection, so Christian baptism means a death of one's old nature, a burial, and a resurrection in which one walks in a newness of life.

LETTERS WRITTEN IN CAPTIVITY

When Paul wrote the letter to the Romans he expressed hope that he would visit the church in that city as soon as arrangements could be made following his journey to the city of Jerusalem. The visit was delayed for about three years and when he did reach the city of Rome he was a prisoner awaiting trial before the court of the emperor. While in Jerusalem he had been arrested on the charge of causing a riot in the Temple. After being in prison for about two years in Caesarea, he was transferred on his own request to be tried in Rome. After spending about three years as a prisoner in Rome he was tried and convicted.

There are seven letters in the New Testament which at times have been credited to Paul on the assumption that he wrote them while a prisoner in Rome. Three of these letters, I and II Timothy, and Titus, are now generally recognized as belonging to a period somewhat later than Paul's death and many New Testament scholars believed the same is true of the one called "the letter to the Ephesians." However in all four of these letters it is possible to recognize the influence of Paul and it can be assumed they were written by disciples of Paul who wrote in accordance with the instruction which they believed he would have given had he been living at that time. The other three letters, Philippians, Philemon, and Colossians are still regarded as genuine letters of Paul although there is some question about the place from which they were written for there is no conclusive evidence to indicate whether it was Rome or Ephesus. Paul had been a prisoner in both of these places.

PHILIPPIANS

The *Letter to the Philippians* is an informal one which Paul sent in response to a gift he had received from the church at Philippi. Knowing that he was in prison and probably in need of material benefits the church had sent one of their number, Epaphroditus, with a gift of money and the intention of staying on to assist Paul in any way that he could. Then Epaphroditus became ill and was forced to return home and Paul sent this letter to the church of Philippi with him.

The letter begins with an expression of thanks for the gift and a prayer for the well-being of the church. With reference to his own personal experience he says that his only desire to be free from prison is that he might be of greater service to the church. He regards it a great privilege to be counted worthy to suffer for the cause of Christ and in this connection he writes a famous hymn concerning Jesus "who though he was in the form of God did not count equality with God a thing to be grasped, but emptied himself, taking the form of a servant, being born in the likeness of men." It is this spirit of humility and service that he commends to the church at Philippi urging that they be of the same mind as that which was manifest in Jesus.

He tells them that Timothy will visit them in the near future and asks that they receive him with kindness. He then interrupts the main course of his letter to throw out a warning against the propaganda being circulated by the Jewish legalists. He reviews in this connection his own experience with Judaism and his conversion to the Christian faith. With a few practical admonitions and a prayer for God's blessing to rest on this church he closes the letter.

PHILEMON

The *Letter to Philemon* was certainly written by Paul. It is a very short letter and has to do with only one topic. Philemon's runaway slave named Onesimus had in some way come in contact with Paul and had come under the influence of the Christian Gospel. The situation was in some respects an embarrassing one for Paul. For a slave to desert his master was considered as a very serious offense and one that was legally punishable by death. Furthermore, it was regarded as the duty of anyone who apprehended a runaway slave to see to it that he was immediately returned to his master. How long Paul had known about Onesimus we are not told. Evidently, it was long enough for him to receive instruction concerning the meaning of the Gospel. Now that the slave has accepted the Christian gospel Paul insists that he must return to his master. His purpose in writing this letter was to request that Philemon not only take him back as his slave but that he shall treat him as a brother in Christ. The letter was written in a most tactful manner for Paul knew that Philemon had a legal right to put him to death. He therefore appealed to his conscience as a Christian brother to recognize that Onesimus was not only a slave but also a child of God. In the eyes of the Roman government he was a criminal deserving of death but as a Christian both he and his master were brothers in Christ.

COLOSSIANS

The *Letter to the Colossians* was addressed to a church which Paul had not visited. A visitor from Colossae named Epaphras had come to see him bringing news and greetings from the Christians in that city. Following a series of conversations with this visitor Paul wrote this letter to the Colossian church. One of the main purposes of the letter was to warn the members concerning a certain dangerous philosophy which was making inroads in that community. The particular doctrine which he apparently had in mind was a form of *Gnosticism* which was a strange mixture of both philosophical and religious ideas. One of their main beliefs was that matter is evil and only spirit is good. They held that the physical world was not created by the supreme being because a perfect deity would not have direct contact with an evil world. It came into existence through the action of a series of intermediary beings whose worship was a necessary means toward human salvation. Paul writes that in Jesus there dwells all the fullness of the Godhead and there is no need for the worship of these intermediary powers. Furthermore he rejects the asceticism as well as the sensual indulgence which was associated with the Gnostic conceptions of salvation.

Commentary

The letters which Paul wrote while a prisoner either at Ephesus or at Rome are the latest which we have from him that have been preserved in the New Testament. They represent his most mature thought concerning the meaning of Christianity and are of especial value for that reason. While he has some things to say with reference to particular problems in local churches his main emphasis has to do with the significance of the life of Jesus in relation to the salvation of human beings and its place in the scheme of the universe as a whole. The letters are of interest too because they reveal the changes which took place in Paul's own thinking during those years after his conversion to Christianity. Perhaps the most significant change that can be noted lies in the fact that he no longer talks about the end of the age in terms of Jewish apocalypticism. The emphasis of his teaching is on the quality of living which is made possible when one's life is transformed by the indwelling presence of the spirit of Christ.

It has been maintained by some writers that in Paul's later years he speaks less about the historic Jesus but more concerning the cosmic Christ.

This can be misleading if it suggests that for Paul the earthly life of Jesus was unimportant or that it did not provide the foundation on which Christianity was built. On the other hand it appears to be true that in Paul's judgment it was the power of the one and only God of the universe, working in Jesus that made his life significant and thus brought to all mankind an opportunity to see how the redemption of humanity can be achieved.

THE SYNOPTIC GOSPELS AND ACTS

The earliest Christians did not have any written records of the life and teachings of Jesus. During the course of his public ministry no one felt the need of making a written account of what he did or what he said. Those who had been close to him would remember what they had seen and heard and they could pass the word on to others. Those who looked upon him as the Messiah believed that he would soon inaugurate the new kingdom and all that was necessary to know about him could be remembered until that time. They were of course sorely disappointed when he was put to death on the cross for it seemed then as though his cause was lost. Afterwards they were convinced that in spite of his death he really was the Messiah who had been promised. With this recognition on their part there was now a new reason for remembering the events of his earthly life. What he had done before his death took on a new meaning in the light of what had happened since that time. There was a need for evidence that would convince unbelievers that he was the Messiah, and the faith of those who already believed in him needed to be confirmed and strengthened. The early Christians all believed that he would soon return to earth and complete the work of preparation for the coming kingdom. An authentic record of his life on earth would be a great help to those who were preparing for his return and with the passing of the years the need was greatly increased.

The fact that the Gospel records were not made until nearly forty years after Jesus' death has often raised questions concerning their reliability. The situation is complicated too by the fact that the Gospel records are not all alike nor is it possible to harmonize completely all of the materials contained in them. They agree on many points but disagree on others. What has been called "the synoptic problem" has to do with finding some hypothesis concerning the origin of these Gospels that will account both for their agreements and for their differences. Many different solutions have been proposed and it must be admitted there is no one of them that is accepted in full by all New Testament scholars. The view that is most widely held maintains that the Gospels in their present form were based very largely on older source materials which were in existence at a time not far removed from the events which they record. If some of the same sources were used by the authors of different gospels and other sources were used only by one author this would go a long way toward explaining both the agreements and the differences which one finds when he compares the different accounts. Since the earliest source materials were written by people who were contemporaries of Jesus and his disciples, this adds considerable weight to their historical reliability.

It is generally agreed that Mark is the oldest of the three synoptic gospels and it was used as one of the sources for each of the other two. The reason for this belief is that the outline of events as they occur in Mark is followed by each of the other biographers and about two thirds of the material found in Mark is also present in both Matthew and Luke.

This suggests very strongly, although it does not prove, that the authors of Matthew and Luke respectively took their materials from Mark. There is reason too for believing that both Matthew and Luke had another source in common. Both of them report a considerable amount of the teachings of Jesus in addition to what is contained in Mark. To account for this material it is assumed that a document composed of Jesus' sayings was in existence and this was another source used along with Mark for the writing of Matthew and of Luke. Scholars refer to this source with the letter *Q* which is the first letter of the German word *Quelle*. Because there is some unique material in Matthew, it is assumed that he used still another source *M* which was not used in any of the other gospels. The same holds true for the Gospel of Luke and scholars use the letter *L* to refer to his special source. This hypothesis concerning the origin of the synoptic gospels appears to be confirmed by the introductory paragraph found in the Gospel of Luke for there it is stated that several lives of Jesus have been written and it is the purpose of the author to write one which will establish the certainty of the things wherein they have been instructed.

THE GOSPEL OF MARK

Summary

Mark, being the oldest of the Gospels, is from the historical point of view the most reliable. The reason for this is not merely that it is closer in point of time to the events which are recorded but there is less interpretation concerning the meaning of these events than one finds in other gospels. The author of this gospel was a Christian named John Mark, a relatively obscure person so far as the New Testament records indicate. He is said to have been a relative of Barnabas who was one of the leaders of the church in Antioch. He accompanied Paul and Barnabas on one of their missionary journeys and he was a companion of Peter during the time when that disciple spent his last years in the city of Rome.

The purpose of Mark's Gospel was to record with as much accuracy as possible the main events in connection with the life and teachings of Jesus. A record of this kind would furnish evidence in support of the belief that Jesus was the true Messiah and by believing in him people could obtain salvation. The fact that this gospel has been preserved in the form in which we have it today testifies to the importance that was attached to it from the beginning. It is a relatively short gospel and most of the material contained in it was reproduced in the gospels which were written later.

The authors of both Matthew and Luke appeared to have included in each of their gospels all that was necessary to be remembered from Mark, in which case the oldest of the gospels would be replaced by later and more complete accounts. The fact that Mark survived these attempts at replacement was probably due to the fact that its origin was regarded as more authentic than the others and then too it was the Gospel which was highly prized by the church at Rome, the one that was destined to become one of the leading churches in the entire Christian movement.

Although the Gospel of Mark became one of the main sources for the writing of Matthew and of Luke it too was based on older source materials. One of these, according to a well authenticated tradition, was an oral source. Papias, one of the early church fathers writing about 140 A.D. tells us that Mark obtained much of the material for his Gospel from the stories related to him by Peter, one of the disciples of Jesus and one who had himself witnessed many of the things which he related. This statement by Papias has been accepted as reliable by most New Testament scholars, for it offers a very reasonable explanation for the contents which are found in the first half of the Gospel. This portion consists of a series of relatively independent stories assembled without reference to the particular time and place of each occurrence or the chronological order of the events. In fact each story is usually introduced with the words "and it came to pass at a certain time." The particular sequence in which the stories are recorded is evidently due to Mark's arrangement of them. The second half of this gospel contains a fairly detailed account of the day by day happenings which took place in or near the city of Jerusalem during the brief period which preceded the arrest, trial, and crucifixion of Jesus.

The Gospel of Mark begins with a brief account of the work of John the Baptist who is referred to as the forerunner of the coming of the Messiah. It was during these days that Jesus came from Nazareth in Galilee and was baptized by John in the river Jordan. Following the baptism, the spirit of God rested upon him and from this time forward he dedicated his life to the work of preparing people for the coming of the kingdom. His public ministry was preceded by a period of temptation which came to him in the wilderness. Soon after the arrest of John the Baptist, Jesus appeared in Galilee preaching the gospel and saying "the kingdom of heaven is at hand." After choosing his disciples he began a vigorous program of evangelization by preaching to the people and healing the sick who were brought to him. Mark was apparently more impressed by the mighty works that Jesus performed than he was by the content of his teaching. More than half of his gospel is devoted very largely to giving an account of the remarkable deeds which Jesus performed. Many of these deeds had to do with healing the sick. He tells of the healing of Simon's mother-in-law who was afflicted with a severe fever. A paralytic who was let down before him by making a hole in the roof was healed and made to walk again. A man with a withered hand was made whole when he encountered Jesus in a synagogue. Unclean spirits were driven out of the Gerasene demoniacs. Jairus' daughter who was at the point of death was made well again. A woman suffering from a hemorrhage was healed and a boy who had been possessed by an unclean spirit from early childhood was restored to health in the presence of his father. In addition to these miracles of healing, Mark reports such incidents as the stilling of the storm on the sea of Galilee, the feeding of the five thousand, the cursing of the fig tree, and other significant events. Most of the miracle stories furnish the occasion for discourses on various themes. The parable of the sower is related together with the interpretation which Jesus made concerning it. It is stated that Jesus made considerable use of parables in his teaching but Mark does not relate very many of them.

As Jesus continued his work in the cities and villages of Galilee, many of the common people heard him gladly. But his plain spoken messages aroused opposition on the part of the elders and rulers among the Jewish people. Some of them took issue with what he was saying or sought to entrap him with clever arguments. Mark reports several of these clashes between Jesus and members of the Pharisee and Sadducee parties. It was in connection with these encounters that Jesus expressed some of his most important teachings. Following the opposition to his work which had developed in the regions of Galilee he journeyed with his disciples into the northwest sections of the country where Tyre and Sidon were located. On his return to Galilee they passed through Caesarea Philippi and it was at this place that the question of his Messiahship was raised with the disciples. Jesus revealed to them that he was the Messiah but told them to say nothing about it. After a brief return to his home country he announced to his disciples that he was going to carry his mission to the Jewish head-quarters in the city of Jerusalem. When he told them what would likely happen to him at the hands of the chief priests and rulers of the nation they were genuinely shocked for they did not believe anything of that kind could possibly happen to the Messiah. They were still hopeful that the time was at hand when he and his followers would enter the promised kingdom.

Following the account of the discussion which took place at Caesarea Philippi, Mark describes the transfiguration which took place when Jesus went up on a mountain accompanied by Peter, James and John. In close connection with the journey to Jerusalem a number of Jesus' discourses are reported. These include the interview with a rich young ruler, the reply given to James and John when they asked for a prominent place in the new kingdom, the discourse given when the money-changers were driven from the Temple, the discussion about paying taxes to the Roman government, the foretelling of the coming destruction of Jerusalem, and the instruction given to the disciples when Jesus ate the Passover meal with them.

The entrance into the city of Jerusalem was a joyous occasion for those who believed he was about to establish the new order of things. But this joy was of short duration for the priests and rulers of the Jews had decided that he was an enemy of their cause and they were determined to get rid of him. Mark reports the experience in the Garden of Gethsemane, the betrayal by Judas, Peter's denial, the trial before Pilate and the story of the crucifixion. The gospel concludes with a brief account of the women who went to the tomb where his body had been placed and found that he had risen from the dead.

Commentary

The Gospel of Mark has several unique characteristics. It reports nothing concerning Jesus' birth, his childhood, or his activities prior to the time when he was baptized by John. This is remarkable in view of the beliefs which were held by many of the early Christians concerning the manner of Jesus' birth and the way in which it was announced in advance of his coming. If these beliefs were fairly common among Christians at the time when Mark wrote, he evidently did not think of them as having sufficient importance to be included in his gospel. For him the real significance of Jesus' career began at the time of his baptism and the decision which followed to devote his life to the work of the kingdom. Throughout the gospel particular emphasis is given to the humanity of Jesus. He becomes weary as other men do after a busy day of hurried activities. Occasionally some question would be raised as to whether he was behaving in a normal manner. At one time during the early ministry in Galilee his friends were very much ·disturbed because of the way he was attracting attention and even the members of his own family were suspicious that he was ill. He did not claim any greatness for himself over that of other people. When an ardent admirer called out to him "Good Master," Jesus promptly rebuked him saying that no one should call him good since that quality belongs only to God.

He never claimed to have any special power that was not available to others. The miracles which he performed were not for the purpose of displaying any power of his own but rather to show how the power of God could be used in and through human lives. He instructed his disciples that the works which he had performed they would do also. In fact he even went farther than that for he told them they would do even greater works than he had done. Further evidence that none of his miraculous works were done in order to attract attention to himself can be seen in the fact that after he had healed someone he would caution them to say nothing about it. A leper came to him one time pleading for help. As soon as Jesus had healed him he said "See that you say nothing to anyone, but go show yourself to the priest," according to the law of Moses. In the synagogue at Capernaum a man with an unclean spirit cried out that Jesus was the "holy one of God." Jesus drove out the unclean spirit but told the man to keep silent about it.

In Mark's Gospel, Jesus does not reveal his Messiahship even to his disciples until they come to Caesarea Philippi. This was shortly before they began the journey to Jerusalem. Even then he cautioned them not to say anything about it. Until then it appears that only Jesus and the demons knew he was the Messiah. Whether Jesus was conscious of it himself from the beginning of his ministry or it was something that developed gradually in his own mind is not made entirely clear. Mark undoubtedly wrote with as much objectivity as possible but viewing the events of Jesus' life from the perspective of what the Christians of thirty or forty years after his death believed about him, he could not refrain from reporting some things in a manner that would harmonize with these later beliefs. An instance of this kind can be seen in the explanation which he gives for the failure of so many people to be convinced by the message which he preached and the deeds he performed. To account for their attitude he refers to a statement used by the prophet Isaiah when he attributed the failure of the Israelite people to listen to the words of Yahweh to the fact that their eyes had been darkened so they could not see the light and their ears had been made dull so they could not understand. It seems to Mark that nothing less than this could have caused the people to reject the program of Jesus which was so obviously in harmony with the divine will. Again it was quite impossible for

Mark to refrain from interpreting many of the sayings of Jesus in the light of what had since taken place in connection with his death, burial and resurrection. Statements which the disciples may not have understood at the time when they were made are now interpreted to have been predictions of what would happen to him in connection with his mission to the city of Jerusalem.

Mark gives a rather full account of Jesus' teachings as well as his activities during those days which preceded his trial and his crucifixion. He tells about the visit of the women to the tomb and their surprise to find that he was risen from the dead. What else he may have said concerning the appearances of Jesus after the resurrection we do not know for the original ending of the book has been lost. The last twelve verses of the gospel as it now appears in our New Testament were not a part of the earliest manuscripts. Even in later manuscripts these verses are not the same. It is evident that they have been added by some editor who recognized that something was lacking in the manuscript which he had and he attempted to complete it. The fact that the original ending of Mark's gospel has been lost is a serious handicap to students of the New Testament for when we omit the verses that have been added the account of the resurrection breaks off in the middle of the story. In fact it breaks off in the middle of a sentence. It would furnish valuable information if we had the remainder of the story since it would be the oldest gospel account of this most important event. What happened to the original ending of the manuscript we do not know. It may have worn off as a result of much handling, but of this we cannot be sure.

THE GOSPEL OF MATTHEW

Summary
Although this gospel was not the first one to be written it has generally been regarded as the most important. It was for this reason that it was placed first in the collection of writings that constitute the New Testament. It contains in addition to materials found in the Gospel of Mark a large number of the sayings and discourses of Jesus and also a group of stories which are not found in any of the other gospels. Because this gospel contains such an extensive account of the teachings of Jesus it has often been regarded as the most authentic and fundamental doctrine of the Christian religion. As one reads through this gospel he is impressed with certain general characteristics which distinguish it from other writings in the New Testament. One of these is the systematic way in which the contents of the gospel have been arranged. For example the document as a whole falls into five distinct divisions with an introductory section preceding the first

one and a concluding section following the last one. Each of the five divisions is composed of a portion of the narrative concerning Jesus' activities together with a group of his teachings. At the end of each division one finds the words "And when Jesus had finished these sayings." This five-fold division of the Gospel of Matthew corresponds in a general way to the divisions found in various parts of the Old Testament.

The sayings and discourses of Jesus are apparently taken in large part from an older document known as "The Sayings of Jesus" or the *Q* source. These are combined with the narrative found in Mark in the following manner. The author of Matthew uses the same sequence of events that are recorded in Mark but at appropriate intervals he interrupts the Marcan narrative and inserts a group of sayings or a number of discourses. An instance of this kind can be seen in what is usually called the "Sermon on the Mount." The materials included in this so-called "Sermon" can be found again in the Gospel of Luke but in this case they are scattered throughout the gospel instead of being grouped together. When Matthew reached that place in the Marcan narrative where Jesus taught the people, he inserts this group of sayings. The organization of these sayings into a single sermon thus appears to be the result of Matthew's arrangement.

Another rather striking characteristic of the Gospel of Matthew is its high regard for the teachings of the Old Testament. There are about fifteen instances reported in which Matthew finds some event in the life of Jesus to be a fulfillment of some prophecy in the Old Testament. Evidently the author of this gospel did not think of Christianity as something that involved a definite break with the Jewish religion. Instead he considered it to be a continuation and fulfillment of that which had been set forth in the literature of the Old Testament. He did not think for a moment that Jesus had come to change or to set aside the requirements of the Mosaic law. Rather, it was his purpose to supplement and interpret those laws in a manner that would be in harmony with their original purpose. In his zeal for showing a close relationship between Jesus and the Old Testament, he appears at times to have made references to incidents in the life of Jesus for no other purpose than that of showing them as fulfillments of Old Testament prophecy. A third characteristic of this gospel is its interest in ecclesiastical affairs. It is the only one of the gospels that makes a direct mention of the church and much of the instruction which is recorded is especially appropriate for particular situations which arose in the Christian churches of the first century.

The gospel begins with a genealogy of Jesus in which his ancestry is traced back as far as Abraham. The ancestry is traced on the side of Joseph although later on it is definitely stated that Joseph was not his father. The genealogy is followed by an account of the visit of the wise men, Herod's attempt to destroy the newborn child, and the flight into Egypt for the child's protection. After the death of Herod the family returned and settled in Nazareth, a town in Galilee. This, according to Matthew, was a fulfillment of Old Testament prophecy.

Following these introductory stories, Matthew continues his gospel by narrating the events in Jesus' public career in the same sequence as they are found in Mark. As mentioned before, this sequence is interrupted at appropriate intervals for the insertion of discourses which Jesus delivered on various occasions. This scheme enables the author to combine the teachings and events in one continuous narrative. While the author of the Gospel of Mark seems to have been impressed most of all with the wonderful deeds which Jesus performed, Matthew places the major emphasis on the marvelous things that Jesus taught. Some of the teachings were spoken directly to the inner group of disciples, but at different times and places he addressed the multitudes. Among them there were many who heard him gladly. Often he spoke in parables for in this way he could communicate his ideas concerning the kingdom of heaven in language which the people could understand because it was drawn from the area of their own experience.

As we have noted before, one of the important issues in the early history of the church was the attitude that Christians should take toward the laws that are recorded in the Old Testament. Paul had insisted that salvation is obtained by faith and not by obedience to laws. This had led some Christians to believe that whether or not these laws should be obeyed was a matter to be decided by the individual's own conscience. Many of the Jewish Christians did not agree with this at all. The author of the Gospel of Matthew appears to have been one of them. According to his version of Jesus' sermon on the mount, it was stated that "it is easier for heaven and earth to pass away than it is for one jot or tittle of the law to fail." Again it was said "if anyone shall break the least of these my commandments and teach men so to do, he shall be least in the kingdom of heaven." It has been maintained by some scholars that this passage was a direct reference to Paul and his followers. Of this we cannot be sure, but it is quite evident from many of the passages in this gospel that Matthew was far more sympathetic toward the religion of Judaism than was true of some of the other writers. In the story of the Canaanite woman who came to him imploring help for her daughter who was possessed by a demon, we are told that Jesus replied by saying "I was sent only to the lost sheep of the house of Israel." When the woman responded by saying "Yes, Lord, yet even the dogs eat the crumbs that fall from their Master's table," Jesus commended her for her faith and healed the daughter.

This, however, represents only one aspect of Matthew's gospel. There are many other passages which indicate that the gospel was for all men and not merely for the Jews. In the parable of the householder who planted a vineyard and left it in charge of his servants while he went into another country, we have a clear indication that the scope of the gospel is inclusive of the Gentiles. In this parable it is stated that the servants were beaten, stoned, and even put to death. Then the householder sent his son and when the tenants saw him they cast him out of the vineyard and killed him. This is clearly a reference to the fact that Jesus had been put to death because of his Jewish enemies. The parable concludes with the words "Therefore I tell you, the kingdom of God will be taken away from you and given to a nation producing the fruits of it."

While Matthew insists that the laws of God are eternal and Christians as well as Jews are under obligation to observe them, he recognizes as clearly as Paul or anyone else that formal obedience in itself is not enough. This is brought out clearly in various parts of the Sermon on the Mount as is indicated by use of the expression "It has been said of old but I say unto you." The point of the contrast in each instance is that not just the overt act but the motive which lies behind it is of primary importance. This is emphasized again in so many of the discussions which Jesus held with the Scribes and Pharisees. Replying to their insistence upon following certain regulations concerning eating and drinking, Jesus made it clear that it was the inner motives of the heart and mind that were of far greater importance than following customs regarding table etiquette.

The early church seems to have entertained two different views concerning the coming of the kingdom of God. Some held that it was strictly a future event. It would be established at the end of the age but not until after the earthly kingdoms had been destroyed. Others held that the kingdom was already present insofar as right principles and motives were established in human hearts. In the Gospel of Matthew there are passages which support each of these views. Perhaps the author believed they could be harmonized by regarding the kingdom within as a kind of preparation for a more complete establishment in the world without at some future time. At any rate there is one chapter in Matthew which presents very clearly the idea that was present in Jewish apocalypticism. It is the chapter in which the sayings of Jesus concerning the coming destruction of the city of Jerusalem is identified as predictions concerning the second coming of Christ and the end of the world. It is here that one finds a group of statements concerning the signs that will reveal when the return of Jesus to this earth will be near at hand. It is said there will be wars and rumors of wars, famines and earthquakes in various places. The sun will be darkened, the moon will not give its light and the stars will fall from heaven. The gospel will be preached in all the world and then the end will come. Jesus will descend to earth on the clouds of heaven in power and great glory. Then will be established the kingdom of God of which there will be no end.

Matthew's Gospel closes with an account of the resurrection and Jesus' appearance to the disciples. We are told that early on the morning of the first day of the week Mary Magdalene and another Mary came to the tomb where Jesus' body had been placed. They were met by an angel who told them Jesus was risen and asked them to look where the body had been. They were commissioned also to go and tell his disciples that he would meet them in Galilee. Since Judas who had betrayed Jesus was dead, there were only eleven disciples left. They met with Jesus as they had been directed to do in Galilee and it was there that he instructed them to "go therefore and make disciples of all nations…and lo, I am with you always to the end of the age."

Commentary

According to a very old tradition the author of the Gospel of Matthew was one of the twelve disciples of Jesus. This view was expressed by Papias toward the middle of the second century. What basis he may have had for this view we do not know. That Jesus did have a disciple who had been a tax-collector is evident from the accounts given in the different gospels. In Mark the name of this tax-gatherer is Levi but in the Gospel of Matthew he is called Matthew. This fact may have had something to do with Papias' statement concerning authorship. However that may be, New Testament scholars of the present day are practically unanimous in their opinion that this gospel was not written by one of Jesus' disciples although it is quite possible that Matthew, the disciple, may have had something to do with one or more of the sources that were used. One of the main reasons for rejecting the traditional view concerning the author is the fact that there are several passages in the gospel itself which indicate quite clearly that it was not written until some time after the destruction of the city of Jerusalem. The date of its composition is generally regarded as somewhere between the years 80 and 85 A.D.

This gospel like the others in the New Testament was evidently based on sources which had been in existence for some time. The two sources on which most of the material was based were *Mark* and the *Logia*. The latter is sometimes called "The Sayings of Jesus" and it is often referred to as the *Q* source. In addition to these, another source, sometimes called *M*, seems to be necessary to account for the unique portions of the gospel. The introductory section for example, contains several stories which are not found in any of the other gospels. These include an account of the birth of Jesus, the visit of the wise men from the East, the meeting of these men with King Herod, Herod's decree calling for the death of male infants, the flight into Egypt, and the settlement in Galilee. Whether these stories were based on oral or written sources we do not know, but they are not found in either Mark or the Logia. All that ancient Israel had looked for with hope and high expectation is now to be fulfilled in the Christian church. Ancient Israel had been given the laws through Moses and now the New Israel has received another and even higher law in the teachings of Jesus. The basis for membership in the new Israel is neither race nor color nor nationality or anything other than the character of individuals who believe in Jesus and put their trust in him. They will come from both Jews and Gentiles and from all parts of the world.

In his selection and use of source materials for the writing of his gospel, Matthew represents different points of view. Some have argued that he was Pro-Jewish in his outlook and others have insisted that he was Pro-Gentile. There are those who would regard him as a thorough-going legalist while others find a strong element of mysticism in his writings. He was, according to some accounts, a disciple of Jewish apocalypticism while others see in him one who believes the kingdom of God will be established gradually in the lives of people. These different interpretations do not constitute evidence that he was confused in his thinking or that he contradicted himself on these various topics. They indicate that he tried to be fair with each of the different points of view recognizing that there was truth to be gained from each of them. The result was the composition of a gospel that presents a balance between opposed conceptions and does so without destroying the element of harmony which brings them all together.

THE GOSPEL OF LUKE

Summary
The Gospel of Luke and the book of Acts are closely related. Both were written by the same author and for the same purpose. Both were addressed to a Christian named Theophilus and they were designed for the purpose of presenting to him a complete and well authenticated narrative of the early history of the Christian movement. In the introductory paragraph of the Gospel, Luke tells us that many lives of Jesus have been written on the basis of reports given by eye witnesses of the events that were recorded. He does not find these narratives satisfactory in all respects

and so he has set himself to the task of examining the records and writing a new account that will establish for all interested parties the certainty of the things about which the Christians have been instructed.

This paragraph is especially informing to students of the New Testament for it describes the way in which the two narratives attributed to Luke came to be written. It informs us that other accounts of the life of Jesus had been written and while Luke was free to draw on them for information he was able to evaluate the materials he wanted to use and to supplement them in whatever manner would seem to him to be most appropriate. In writing his Gospel he did something more than piece together bits of information which he had gathered from different sources. His own contribution included selection and organization of these materials along with whatever interpretation was necessary to make a complete and unified narrative.

We can be quite certain that Luke made use of at least three different sources. These include the Gospel of Mark, the *Q* source or Sayings of Jesus, and a third one which is usually designated as *L* to distinguish it from the ones used by other biographers. The Gospel of Matthew may have been in existence by the time Luke wrote his account but there is nothing which indicates that he knew anything about it or made any use of it. Luke had been a companion of Paul and he was quite familiar with the different interpretations of the life of Jesus held by members of the Christian community. It was his purpose to minimize the differences between the various groups and thus promote harmony within the church. He was aware, too, of the criticisms that were being made concerning Christianity on the part of those who were outside the church. He was especially concerned to make an effective reply to those who had claimed that Jesus was a revolutionist and hence an enemy of the Roman government. By giving to his readers an authentic account of the life and teachings of Jesus he could show wherein the charges made against him were false. He was quite sure that if people only knew the kind and sympathetic way in which he met people they would be won by the attractive power of his wonderful personality. Luke possessed rare ability as a writer and it has often been said that his gospel is in many respects the most appealing of all those in the New Testament.

In the opening chapters of this gospel one finds a number of stories having to do with the birth and childhood of Jesus. These include the announcements made to Zechariah and to Mary concerning the births of John and of Jesus. The story of the shepherds who were watching their flocks by night and who came to worship the newborn child is related. Also we have an account of the journey of Joseph and Mary to Bethlehem and the child being wrapped in swaddling clothes and placed in a manger "because there was no room for them in the inn." After eight days the child was circumcised and when he was taken to the temple he was blessed by Simeon and again by Anna the prophetess. None of these stories are reported in the other gospels and we cannot be sure whether Luke learned about them from an older source or from oral traditions. Luke has recorded the only story we have in the New Testament about Jesus' boyhood. When he was twelve years of age he went up to Jerusalem with his parents to attend the feast of the Passover. On the way home when the parents discovered that he was not with them, they returned to the Temple and found him involved in a profound discussion with prominent Jewish rabbis.

After the introductory chapters in which these incidents are reported Luke follows the outline of events as they were recorded in the Gospel of Mark. He does not follow Mark's narrative as closely as was done by Matthew. Occasionally he leaves out some material and substitutes an item of his own. An instance of this kind can be seen in his omission of Jesus' proclamation at the beginning of his Galilean ministry and substituting for it an illustration of his preaching in the synagogue at Nazareth. Luke includes in his gospel a considerable amount of the teachings of Jesus which are not recorded in the other ones. If he and Matthew both used the same source Q, it is evident that Luke used more material from it than did Matthew. It is in Luke alone that we find the parables of the Good Samaritan, the Publican and the Pharisee who went up to the Temple to pray, the rich man and Lazarus, the lost coin, the prodigal son, the unjust steward, the rich fool who would tear down his barns and build greater in order that he might store his goods, and the story of Zacchaeus who climbed a tree in order that he might see Jesus. Each of these parables and stories illustrates what Luke regards as an essential characteristic of the work of Jesus. He was not trying to raise opposition to the Roman government nor was he lacking in sympathy or understanding of those whom the Jews have regarded as foreigners. He places the highest value on good character regardless of one's race or nationality. While many of the Jews looked with disfavor on the Samaritans, Luke emphasizes the fact that of the ten lepers who were healed it was only the one who was a Samaritan who came back to express his gratitude for what had been done. And again in the parable of the man who fell among thieves on the road to Jericho it was a Samaritan who befriended him and saw to it that he was given proper care.

Throughout this gospel, emphasis is placed on the fact that Jesus was a friend not simply to the Jews but to the Samaritans and to the so-called "outcasts" from different races and nationalities. Chapters 9-18 have often been referred to as Luke's "long insertion" for it is at this point that he departs from the sequence of events in Mark and introduces a section which includes much of the most valued portions of Jesus' teachings. It is here that we have a report of Jesus sending out the "seventy" to carry the message of the kingdom to different places. The number "seventy" is especially significant for in the Jewish Torah it was used to refer to all the nations of the earth. Luke wants to make it clear that Jesus' mission was for all mankind and not just for the Jews. In the story which describes the conversation between Jesus and Zacchaeus, we have the statement "the Son of Man came to seek and to save the lost." Again in the introductory chapters of the gospel where Luke, like Matthew, traces the genealogy of Jesus, we find the same emphasis on the universality of Jesus' mission. While Matthew traced the ancestry back to Abraham who was regarded as the father of the Hebrew people, Luke traces it back to Adam, who was the father of all mankind.

In reporting Jesus' discourses with his disciples concerning the destruction of Jerusalem and the end of the world, Luke does not emphasize the nearness of the event so much as the other evangelists did. Toward the end of the gospel he describes the events leading up to the crucifixion stressing the point of Jesus' innocence of any wrongdoing toward either the Jews or the Roman government. Pilate the Roman governor declares that he is innocent of any crime and a Roman centurion protests against his execution with the words "Certainly this man was innocent." The gospel closes with an account of the resurrection and the subsequent meetings of Jesus with the disciples and others. It is while two of the disciples are walking to the village of Emmaus that Jesus joins them but they do not recognize him until he sat at a table with them and blessed the food which they were about to eat. Later he meets with the eleven disciples in Jerusalem and overcomes their suspicions by showing his hands and feet. They cooked some fish and he partook of the food with them. Then follows a farewell discourse to the disciples and he gives them instruction concerning what they should do. Afterwards they go out together as far as Bethany and after blessing the disciples, Jesus departed from them.

Commentary

If the Gospel of Matthew could be called the Jewish Gospel because of its leanings toward ideas that were typically Jewish, there is an equal amount of evidence for calling the Gospel of Luke the Gentile Gospel. Actually neither gospel is purely Jewish or purely Gentile in its account of the life and teachings of Jesus. But it is fairly obvious in the case of each of them that the authors have been influenced by the point of view with which they have been associated. Luke had been a companion of Paul who came to be known in Christian circles as the Apostle to the Gentiles. His interpretation of Christianity as a universal religion had done much to eliminate the barriers between Jews and Gentiles. He had emphasized the idea that all men are sinners and in need of salvation. Jesus was, for him, the supreme example of what the power of God can do in a human life regardless of one's race, nationality, or creed. This point of view had evidently made a deep impression on Luke and it is reflected throughout the various parts of his gospel. One sees it first of all in his account of the genealogy of Jesus which is traced to Adam rather than to Abraham, thus indicating that Jesus was representative of the entire human race rather than simply a member of the Hebrew race. It is seen too in the attitude taken by Jesus toward the Samaritans, the Romans, and others who were outside the Jewish fold. When a contrast is shown between Jews and Gentiles, it is often the Gentile who is presented in the more favorable light. One sees this illustrated in the story of the Publican and the Pharisee, both of whom went up to the Temple to pray but it was only the Publican who was commended for the attitude which he expressed. Following the journey into the northwest country, woes were pronounced on Capernaum and other Jewish communities and it was stated that "it shall be more tolerable in the judgment for Tyre and Sidon than for you." This does not mean that for Luke the Jewish people have been rejected but rather that membership in the kingdom of God is dependent on the quality of one's living rather than racial or religious background.

Paul has often been referred to as a Christian mystic because of his conviction that salvation comes only by a union of the individual and God. When the spirit of God dwells in the human heart and mind as it did in the person of Jesus, then one belongs to the kingdom. Jewish apocalypticism had regarded the coming of the kingdom as a future event when the Son of Man would descend from heaven. In the Gospel of Luke we find a blending of these two ideas. Luke, the same as Matthew, made use of the apocalyptic section in Mark's Gospel but with certain modifications. The nearness of the event is not stressed so much and Luke recognizes that there is a sense in which the kingdom is already present. "Say not lo here, or lo there, for the kingdom of heaven is within you." When Jesus was accused of casting out demons because he was exercising the power of a greater demon he replied "But if it is by the finger of God that I cast out demons, then the kingdom of God has come upon you." In the story concerning Jesus and Zacchaeus, the coming of the kingdom is portrayed in a similar manner. When Zacchaeus stood up and said "the half of my goods I give to the poor, and if I have defrauded anyone of anything I restore it fourfold." Jesus replied by saying "Today salvation has come to this house." These passages as well as many others which might be mentioned indicate that Luke was thoroughly in sympathy with Paul's mystical conception of the Christ that lives and abides in human hearts. Yet he does not abandon the apocalyptic conception of the coming of an end of the age, but the emphasis is placed on the quality of living which alone can prepare one for the coming of the great event in the future.

As nearly as we can determine, the Gospel of Luke was written toward the end of the first century, probably between the years 85-90 A.D. By this time Christianity was fast becoming a world-wide movement. Starting in Jerusalem it had spread into the surrounding territory and had reached as far west as the city of Rome. With the increasing numbers of Christians, the movement was not only attracting attention but it was encountering opposition from several different quarters. Rumors had been circulated to the effect that the founder of the movement was a dangerous character who was trying to overthrow the government. Luke was by nature a peacemaker and he was anxious to show that Jesus was not the type of person that these critics supposed he was. He therefore takes particular pains to point out that he had no quarrel at all with the Roman government. Pilate finds in him no fault at all. A Roman centurion declares that he was innocent and while it was true that Pilate finally consented to his crucifixion it was not until he had been pressured by the Jews that he did so. Jesus' whole ministry had been conducted in a quiet and peaceful manner. He had been the friend of the poor and the outcast and with no political ambitions of his own or any intention of trying to interfere with the orderly processes of government.

Writing from the point of view of the Christian church toward the end of the first century, Luke is convinced that the characteristics of the movement which were then being emphasized had been present from the very beginning. He shows, for example that the opposition to Jesus and the work he was doing was present during the early ministry in Galilee. It was demonstrated in their reactions to the sermon he preached in the synagogue at Nazareth. They continued their harassment throughout his entire public career and the cause of it was their resentment of the criticisms he had made of their formalism and hypocrisy. Finally they were determined to get rid of him in order to silence his criticisms and as a means toward this end they had invented the false charges concerning his disloyalty to the government. Again Luke shows the broad humanitarian character of his work which was manifested from the first in his attitude toward the Samaritans and others whom the Jews had regarded as their enemies. He never failed to commend those who had an humble and contrite heart and it made no difference whether they were Jews or Gentiles. At the time of Luke's writing it was the spirit of the Christ that was regarded as the guiding factor in the life of the Christian church. That this was only a continuation of what had been present all along is shown by Jesus' repeated references to the Spirit of God throughout the period of his public ministry. What he had taught was now seen to be in harmony with what the church believed. Many of the statements which had been attributed to Jesus were now interpreted in the light of what had happened since, implying at least in some instances that they had been intended as definite predictions of what was going to take place.

THE BOOK OF ACTS

Summary

The Book of Acts is a continuation of the narrative which Luke began in his Gospel. It is especially important for the student of the New Testament since it was the first history of the Christian church to be written. It has to do with that very vital period in Christian history between the resurrection of Jesus and the death of the apostle Paul. This was the time when Christian ideas and beliefs were being formulated and when the organization of the church into a world-wide movement was being developed. It is only in the light of this background that one can understand the writing of the Gospels as well as the other New Testament literature which followed.

The book has been called "The Acts of the Apostles" but this is really a misnomer since it has very little to say concerning most of the original twelve. The activities of Peter are described at some length and mention is made of John and of Philip but more than half of the book is about Paul and his connection with the Christian movement. Scholars are somewhat divided in their opinions concerning the authorship of parts of the book. There can be no question about Luke being the author of parts of the book but the inclusion of what has been called the "we sections" raises some question about the persons to whom the pronoun "we" refers. Does it mean that someone other than Luke is also involved in the reports which are made? While no definite answer can be given to this question it seems highly probable that Luke was the author of the original book but that the work of editors and redactors were added before it reached the final form in which we have it today.

The book contains twenty-eight chapters. Of these the first twelve report events between the time of Jesus' last meeting with his disciples and the beginning of Paul's work as a Christian missionary. The remaining sixteen chapters describe Paul's activities beginning with his mission to the church at Antioch and ending with an account of his residence in Rome as a prisoner of the Roman government. The events recorded in the first section of the book include such topics as the ascension of Jesus into heaven, the choosing of a disciple to replace Judas who had betrayed Jesus, the feast of Pentecost in which we hear of the so-called gift of tongues, Peter's sermon delivered on that occasion, the arrest of Peter and John in the Temple at Jerusalem, the sin of Ananias and Sapphira, the stoning of Stephen, Philip's meeting with the eunuch and the baptism which followed, the story of Paul's conversion on the road to Damascus, and Peter's visit with Cornelius, the centurion. In addition to giving us some insight concerning the early activities of the Christian community these accounts are especially valuable in that they tell us about the beliefs which Christians held concerning Jesus prior to the writing of the Gospels.

In Paul's letter to the church at Corinth we have the earliest written summary of the Christian faith. He mentions in this connection that he had received no direct revelation concerning the facts pertaining to the life of Jesus and their significance for the Christian faith but he is passing on to the members of that church what has been related to him by others. From this statement we would infer that the essential beliefs of the Christian community about Jesus had already been formulated and were included in the preaching which had taken place prior to that time. The first section of the book of Acts reports several different sermons which give us definite information about these beliefs. They constitute the *kerygma* or the primitive gospel which was proclaimed by the early Christians before any written records had been made. For example we are told about Peter's sermon to a group of about one hundred and twenty persons, another sermon which he delivered on the day of Pentecost, and a third one which he preached in Jerusalem standing on Solomon's porch in front of the Temple. Stephen's sermon at the time of his stoning is reported at considerable length and we are told of Philip's instruction to the eunuch whom he baptized and again of Peter's discourse with Cornelius and his report to the Christian leaders at Jerusalem. In the last section of Acts a number of Paul's sermons are recorded in considerable detail. From these records it is possible to reconstruct with a fair degree of accuracy the main contents of the *kerygma* or earliest preaching of the Christian church.

The story of the stoning of Stephen throws some light on those factors in Paul's experience which led to his conversion on the road to Damascus. From chapter 13 on to the end of the book we have a somewhat detailed account of Paul's missionary journeys and his experiences with the different churches. In chapter 15 we have a report concerning the Jerusalem council in which the issue concerning circumcision was discussed. The account which Luke gives with reference to the results of this meeting does not agree in all details with the account given of the same meeting in Paul's letter to the Galatians. Since Paul was a participant in the council and Luke was giving what might be called a second-hand account, the preference must be given to the one in the Galatian letter. Luke was a strong believer in Christian unity and in this instance, as well as in others which might be mentioned, he was anxious to minimize the differences between conflicting views. It seemed to him that the question had to be settled in a manner that was satisfactory to everyone. In the light of the controversy which developed later, it seems that he was mistaken.

The remainder of the book of Acts describes Paul's visit to Macedonia. While in the city of Philippi he and his companion Silas were thrown into prison. After an earthquake had shaken the prison they were released and at Paul's insistence they were given a police guard until they were safely out of the city. The experiences at Athens and at Corinth are related and an account is given of Paul's work at Ephesus where he stayed for a considerable period of time, probably from two to three years. The occasion for his last visit to the city of Jerusalem was the collection of gifts from the various churches which he wished to give for the relief of the Christians who were poor in that city. Trouble broke out while he was there and he was accused of starting a riot in the Temple. Paul spoke at some length in his own defense. Forty men had entered into a plot to kill Paul, but a friend had warned him and he appealed to the Roman officer for protection. The officer heeded his request and he was given asylum at Caesarea which was the seat of the Roman government in Palestine. It was here that hearings were held before Felix and Agrippa and at each of them Paul was given an opportunity to speak in his own defense. At his request he was permitted to go to Rome in order that his case might be tried in Caesar's court. On the voyage to Rome he was shipwrecked but eventually he did get to Rome where he was accorded a considerable amount of liberty even though he was still a prisoner. After a time he was tried, convicted, and executed.

Commentary

Luke's purpose in the writing of the book of Acts was to trace the expansion of the Christian movement from its earliest beginnings to the time when it had reached world-wide proportions. He was keenly aware of the way in which it was being attacked by enemies of the movement and he wanted to present the story of its development in its most favorable light. It was quite impossible to write a complete history of the movement but he was able to select those events which he regarded as the more important ones and these would be sufficient to characterize the movement as a whole. Having been a companion of Paul he was more familiar with the work which he had been doing than he was with the activities of other Christian leaders. Then too, he was an admirer of Paul and he realized the significance of his work in bringing the Gospel to various cities outside of Palestine. He was deeply appreciative of the point of view held by the Jewish Christians who conceived of Christianity as a further development of

Judaism instead of being a movement which was entirely separate. He wanted to emphasize the agreements rather than the differences among those groups whose ideas frequently clashed with one another. In this respect he was a kind of trouble-shooter of the early Christian movement. We do not know just what source materials he had for his writing. Some things he had observed himself, and it is quite possible that he may have kept a diary from which he extracted materials that were useful for his narrative. Presumably he had access to other manuscripts as well, and some of the things he reported had been obtained by direct conversation with others. It is true that many things have been omitted and he was not completely unbiased in all that he wrote. Indeed that is not the case with any historian. But with all these limitations Luke produced a remarkable piece of work and its inclusion in the New Testament contributes a great deal toward a better understanding of the rest of the literature.

The early Christian sermons which he summarized and recorded form to a very great extent the basis for a reconstruction of the *kerygma* and it is from this point of view that the Gospel records were made. Luke's account of the way in which Christianity made its way among the gentiles without discarding the more vital points of Judaism did much toward the establishment of unity and those Christians whose backgrounds so far as religious training was concerned were quite different. The account of Paul's arrest in the city of Jerusalem and the trials which followed was a clear vindication of the man in the eyes of any impartial reader. The end of the book is somewhat disappointing because one would expect to read about his trial in Caesar's court but instead the account ends rather abruptly. Some people think Luke may have intended to write a third volume of his history, but was unable to do it. Of this we cannot be certain. However, we are indebted to him in no small measure for the two accounts of Christianity which he did write.

PASTORAL LETTERS

Summary
Three short letters in the New Testament are addressed to Christian pastors. Traditionally they were attributed to Paul on the assumption that he wrote them while he was a prisoner in Rome. Two of these were addressed to Timothy, a young man whose parents had become Christians prior to the time when Paul visited them in the town of Lystra which was in Asia Minor. Timothy joined Paul in his missionary activities and continued to minister to the churches after Paul had become a prisoner in Rome. The third letter was addressed to Titus, a young man born of Gentile parents who became a Christian and who was one of the delegation sent

by the church at Antioch to accompany Paul and Barnabas when they went to Jerusalem for a meeting of the Council. During Paul's missionary journeys, he was sent on two different occasions to the church at Corinth to help in the settlement of difficult problems which had arisen in that congregation. Nothing is said in either of the letters to Timothy about the occasion for writing but in the letter to Titus mention is made of the fact that Paul was in prison.

It is now generally agreed among New Testament scholars that these letters, at least in their present form, were not written by Paul. The reasons for this opinion are based partly on the style and vocabulary used, for they are quite different from what we find in the older letters which Paul did write. There is an absence too of the theological conceptions which Paul used so frequently, but the major reason is that the ecclesiastical order which these letters presuppose did not exist in Paul's day. The letters were probably written by someone who was an admirer of Paul and who wrote the kind of instruction which he believed Paul would approve.

LETTERS TO TIMOTHY

I Timothy was written for the purpose of doing two things. The first one was to give instruction in worship and in church administration. The second one was to warn against false teachings that were creeping into the churches. With reference to worship there were certain forms to be observed and certain types of conduct which should be strictly avoided. Since it was necessary for both bishops and deacons to be appointed in the churches, it was highly important that these offices be respected and for careful attention to be given to the selection of men to fill them. The bishop must be above reproach, temperate, dignified, of a peaceful disposition and one who is not a lover of money. The deacons, too, must be men of serious mind, free from greed, and conscientious in all of their activities. They should be tested first and only those who prove to be blameless should be permitted to serve in that office.

The letter contains a special warning against the false beliefs and practices that were associated with Gnosticism. Particular attention is directed toward some of these. For example he specifies the asceticism which was advocated by some Gnostics in their efforts to overcome the demands of the physical body, and the opposite method which was urged by others who taught that indulgence in various forms of sensuality would accomplish the same purpose. Both asceticism and over-indulgence were based on the Gnostic conception that matter is evil and only that which is spirit is good. Christians were also warned against being misled by the godless and silly myths that formed a part of the special kind of knowledge which Gnostics regarded as essential for salvation. The letter expresses reproof toward those who try to make a profit out of religion and it contains instructions concerning the attitude which Christians should take in their dealings with widows, presbyters, and slaves.

II Timothy is a letter written by an experienced missionary to a younger colleague urging him to recognize that endurance is one of the main qualities that is essential for a successful preacher of the gospel. Evidently, situations had developed within the churches that were especially difficult for the Christian pastor. Timothy is urged to stand firm and to rekindle the gift of God that is within him. He must be willing to bear hardships when necessary and to conduct himself as a good soldier for God. He needs both courage and humility to perform the tasks that have been assigned to him. In combating false doctrine he must refrain from all that is ignoble, showing that he is a sound workman rightly dividing the words of truth. He can draw help and inspiration from the example of Paul who is now at the end of his career and about to receive a crown of righteousness. The letter closes with personal greetings to the members of the church.

LETTER TO TITUS

The *Letter to Titus* contains three chapters. It is similar in content to the first letter addressed to Timothy. It specifies the qualifications for the office of bishop and gives instruction for the appointment of elders in the church. Since the bishop is God's steward he must be blameless, hospitable, able to control his temper, and he must not be arrogant, self-indulgent, or intemperate. He must have a firm grasp of the word of God and be able to give instruction in sound doctrine. In dealing with the men and women who are members of the church, the bishop or elder in charge must train them to be serious, temperate, sensible and to be sound in faith, love, and steadfastness. Women are to be instructed to love their husbands and children. Younger men are to be taught to control themselves. Slaves should be taught obedience to their masters and finally Christians are to avoid hatred and wrangling. They should be encouraged to manifest meekness, gentleness, and courtesy which is made possible by God's mercy in Christ.

LETTER TO THE EPHESIANS

The *Letter to the Ephesians* can scarcely be called a pastoral letter, since it was not addressed to a particular church leader giving him advice on how to conduct his work. We have no proof that Paul wrote the letter although it was supposed for a long time that he did. The evidence contained in the letter itself suggests very strongly that it was written sometime after Paul's death, probably by one of his disciples who may have wanted it to appear that Paul wrote it because of the added prestige that this would give to it. There are no personal greetings to particular individuals in this letter although Paul had been with the church in Ephesus for a period of about three years and would certainly have formed some close personal friendships.

No mention is made of the Jewish controversy over legalism which is found in nearly all of Paul's letters and the most convincing argument of all that Paul did not write the letter is the fact that reference is made to the "apostles and prophets" as the foundation of the church while Paul always insisted that the church had no foundation other than Jesus Christ. The letter was evidently written for the churches at a time when church organization had proceeded quite beyond the point it had reached while Paul was still living.

Two main themes are expounded in the letter. One of them is the unity of all things in Christ and the other one is the Christian church which is the visible symbol here on earth of that unity. The author of the letter asserts that in the life of Jesus there is revealed the divine purpose which has existed from the creation of the world. The cause of all the disunity which has been in evidence over the centuries was not any flaw in the creative process but it has been due to man's sin. The spirit of God which was made manifest in the life of Jesus here on this earth has shown how this disunity can be overcome and the original harmony restored. With the overcoming of evil in the lives of human beings there is achieved a unity not only between man and God but a cosmic unity which unites all things on earth and in heaven. There is therefore no need for any worship of powers that are intermediary between heaven and earth as had been taught by Gnostics of that day.

Again it is through the person of Christ that unity has been achieved between Jews and Gentiles. The Gentiles who at one time had been separated from the people of God and who were in bondage to the evil powers of the universe were now offered salvation and have been made one with the children of God through Jesus the Christ. A new household of God has been created through the preaching of the apostles and the Christian prophets. The church has been called into being to bear witness to the divine purpose and to knit together men from all races and nations into a single community in which God dwells through his Spirit. The letter closes with ethical instructions for the members of the church to the end that this unity may be achieved. Since the church is the visible body of Christ it must grow strong in the bonds of love as it fulfills its mission in the world.

Commentary

Although the Pastoral letters can scarcely be attributed directly to Paul they do contain passages which have every indication of Pauline authorship. Certainly his influence can be seen in them even though these passages are now combined with other material which seemed to be appropriate for the conditions which existed in the churches at the time when the letters were written. They are especially valuable from the historical point of view since they reveal the beginnings of that type of church organization which, with modifications, has persisted even to the present time.

From the religious point of view the letters are in one sense inferior to the ones written by Paul. The chief difference lies in the fact that they do not show the close connection between Christian faith and Christian living which was so characteristic of Paul's writings. He never failed to point out that the fruits of the spirit would always be expressed in the quality of one's daily living. Faith was something that gripped the entire personality and the results could be seen in one's actions as well as in his attitudes and beliefs. The pastoral letters emphasize two duties that are incumbent on all Christians. One is to believe certain things and the other is to do certain things, but the way in which these are related is not set forth in the manner which Paul had made so clearly in his letters to the churches.

In spite of this weakness, the letters do set forth a high standard for Christian living. They do contain practical instruction for meeting the problems which arise in daily living and their message was something that could be understood even by those who were not so theologically inclined.

OPEN LETTERS TO THE CHURCHES

Summary

The era which followed immediately after the death of the Apostles is usually designated as the early post-apostolic period. It was a critical time in the history of the Christian Church, for its membership had spread to various parts of the world, and in both size and influence the movement was growing. Since the early pioneers of the movement were no longer living it was necessary to recruit leadership from among the newer members. Here problems were constantly arising and there was need for guidance in dealing with them. It was for the purpose of helping toward meeting this need that a number of relatively short documents were produced and distributed among the churches. Because the problems with which they were concerned were not confined to any one local community, they were written for the church at large. It is for this reason that they have sometimes been designated as the *Catholic* epistles. Although most of them have by tradition been credited either to one of the apostles or someone closely associated with them, the evidence would seem to indicate that all of them belong to the post-apostolic period. When they first appeared they were anonymous but in later years they were attributed to individuals who had been prominent in the beginnings of the Christian movement. This would give to the documents an added prestige and it was not at all uncommon in the ancient world for this type of thing to be done. Included in this group of writings are one letter attributed to James, two to the apostle Peter, three to John the disciple of Jesus, and one to a Christian named Jude.

I Peter is one of the more important letters in this group. It was written primarily for the benefit of Christians who were suffering severe persecution at the hands of the Roman government. It will be recalled that the book of *Revelations* was written for a similar purpose. There were, however, some important differences which led to the writing of this letter. *Revelations* was addressed to the seven churches in Asia Minor because it was in that locality that emperor worship was threatening to destroy all those who refused obedience to its demands. When *I Peter* was written this type of "fiery ordeal" had become world-wide and Christians wherever they might be living were called upon in the name of the government to renounce their allegiance to Christ. Even to be called a Christian was considered to be sufficient grounds for condemnation. This situation did not exist prior to the reign of the emperor Domitian or during the last decade of the first century. This is one of the main reasons for assigning the letter to a period which came after the death of Peter the apostle.

Although there is relatively little of a theological nature in this letter it sets forth a very high standard of Christian living. In contrast with the book of *Revelations* with all of its bitter condemnations of the Roman empire, *I Peter* urges the Christians to take a different attitude toward their suffering. The trials and afflictions which have come upon them are for the purpose of testing their faith. Christian character is not developed by living under conditions of ease and comfort. It is only by meeting difficult situations and conquering them that one becomes spiritually strong. Just as gold must be tried in the fire until the dross is burned out of it, so Christians must be tried in order to bring about the perfection of their character. Besides this, Christians have the example of Jesus to follow, and they should consider it a privilege to be counted worthy to suffer even as he did for the glory of God. To endure with patience even to the end is a goal worthy of attainment. However, through it all the Christian should be encouraged because he knows the suffering will last for only a short time and he has the "lively hope" of a glorious future of which there will be no end.

One interesting passage in this letter refers to the time when Jesus preached to the "spirits in prison." This passage has given rise to much speculation and it did have something to do with the formulation of the apostles' creed in later centuries. Since Christians believed and taught that faith in Jesus as the Christ was essential for salvation, the question arose concerning the fate of those who had died without having the opportunity to know or even hear of Jesus. Could they be saved? If they could not then the justice of God would be brought into question and if they could, faith in Jesus was not essential for salvation. It was in order to meet this dilemma that the idea to which this passage refers was developed.

According to this conception Jesus, between the time of his death and his resurrection, had descended to Sheol where according to ancient Hebrew tradition all persons went after death, and there he preached to all those who had died, thus giving to them a chance to accept or to reject his message. It was a strange notion but it offered a kind of solution to a very difficult problem. The influence of this idea can be recognized in that portion of the creed which says, "he descended into hell."

The Letter of James appears to have been written at a time near the close of the first century. Although attributed to James who was the brother of Jesus, the contents of the letter indicate a conception of religion quite different from the one which James the head of the Jerusalem council supported. It therefore seems probable that the letter was written by another James who had a message which he regarded as appropriate for the churches at that time. Paul had emphasized the importance of faith as the means of salvation and he had disparaged those who believed it could be obtained by obedience to the laws of God. This had been interpreted by many to mean that nothing mattered so long as one believed that Jesus was the Christ. The law was no longer binding and Christians could follow their own inclinations in matters of conduct. It was for the purpose of correcting this notion that the letter of James was written.

The author of the letter defines religion that is "pure and undefiled" strictly in terms of ethical conduct. As he sees it the actions of individuals are far more important than the mere content of one's intellectual beliefs. He insists that "faith without works is dead." Furthermore the standard of goodness is obedience of the laws of God. It is in obeying what he calls "the perfect law of liberty" that individuals find their true freedom. Anyone who breaks one of the commandments is guilty of all. It is evident, however, that he has in mind the moral rather than the ritualistic commandments for he sees no virtue in mere formalism. It is in helping the poor and the needy and maintaining an humble attitude that the Christian religion is exemplified. He has much to say about the harm that may arise from gossip and careless use of the tongue. The rich, too, are severely criticized for hoarding their wealth instead of using it to meet the needs of their fellowmen. The letter ends rather abruptly but with an emphasis upon the type of ethical conduct which should always characterize the life of a true Christian.

I John is a short homily written by a Christian elder. Its purpose was to instruct the churches concerning a problem that was becoming more serious as time continued. Christians had been taught that after Jesus left this earth, the Spirit of God would guide and direct the movement. The spirit that had been present in Jesus had spoken through the apostles and now that they were gone it continued to speak through other individuals.

As a result of this belief many persons claimed to be the medium through which God's truth was being revealed to the churches. All sorts of ideas were being advanced by individuals who insisted that the spirit had revealed to them whatever it was that they were advocating. Unless some restraint could be placed on individuals who made such claims the situation would soon become chaotic. This letter proposes that certain tests be applied before accepting anyone who claims to have been informed by the Spirit of God.

One of these tests is doctrinal in character. It states that anyone who denies that Jesus the Christ has come in the flesh is not of God. This test was directed especially against that form of the Gnostic philosophy known as Doceticism. They had accepted the idea of Jesus' divinity but they had denied his humanity insisting that he had only appeared to have a physical body. The other test was an ethical one. Those who claimed to be "possessed" by the Spirit of God must be examined before being accepted in the church. If their conduct does not harmonize with the ethical teachings of Jesus they are not to be received into church fellowship. The church is warned against the many false prophets and teachers who have arisen and they are urged to apply the test of brotherly love as well as that of obedience to the commandments of God.

II John is a very short letter written by the same elder to a sister church which he designates as the "elect lady." The letter indicates that the false teachers who deny that Jesus Christ has been present in the flesh have made inroads in the church and are producing a serious schism. The church is warned concerning these deceivers and told to show no hospitality toward them.

III John is another letter from this elder. The church is commended for receiving Gaius who has performed important services for the brethren. They are warned about a certain man named Diotrephes who has spoken slanderously of the Elder and tried to have him put out of the church. Again some of the tests of a godly man are enumerated.

II Peter is attributed in the superscription to Simon Peter the disciple of Jesus. Since the letter contains many indications of authorship later than the death of the apostle it is assumed that the subscription was used for the purpose of giving authority to the message which it contains. The letter warns against those persons who are skeptical concerning the coming of the Day of the Lord. The churches are encouraged to hold fast the faith they have received for as it was in the days of Noah so it will be again when the Son of Man shall come. The day of the Lord will come as a thief in the night. Therefore, it behooves all Christians to live in readiness for it.

The letter of *Jude* who speaks of himself as a servant of Jesus Christ and a brother of James, contains a single chapter. The purpose of the letter is similar to that of *II Peter*. In fact there are some scholars who maintain that this letter was written first and parts of it were copied and expanded by the author of *II Peter*. It is a polemical tract written to warn the churches against false doctrines that were gradually making their ways within the membership of the churches. It is directed primarily against Gnosticism with its teaching concerning a strange kind of wisdom which is expressed in mysterious language. Their dualistic conception of good mind but evil body is out of line with Christian doctrine and should be rejected and the same holds for their conception of Jesus as one who only appeared to have a human body. The author quotes from the book of *Enoch* which was one of the Jewish apocalypses that is included in the Pseudepigrapha of the Old Testament.

Commentary

The letters included in their list are valuable as source materials for reconstructing the history of the early church. They tell us about the problems both theological and practical with which the church had to contend. Some of these letters have little value apart from this history. This is especially true of *Jude, II Peter, II and III John*. But something more can be said for the other three. *I Peter* sets forth a conception of the Christian life that is attractive and ennobling. It tells how the hardships and trials of human life may become a means toward the development of Christian character. It sets before the Christian a glorious hope that may serve as a guide and inspiration. The letter of James will always be remembered for its ethical conception of religion at its best. It serves, too, to correct the faulty notion that Christian faith is merely a matter of intellectual belief. It shows rather that true faith in the Christian gospel will be expressed in actions as well as in what one thinks. *I John* presents a conception of Christianity which has much in common with the Gospel of John. It makes love the central factor in the Christian life.

THE LETTER TO THE HEBREWS

Summary

After the Christian community had been in existence for a few decades the enthusiasm which had characterized its earlier years began to wane. The expected return of Jesus had not taken place, opposition to the movement had developed from different quarters, and doubts were beginning to arise concerning any permanent significance which it might have over other religious sects and parties. To counteract these tendencies and to strengthen the faith of the Christians who were associated with the new movement was the chief purpose of this letter. The author is unknown although many guesses have been made concerning his identity. It has been attributed to the apostle Paul and in many editions of the New Testament this idea is expressed in the title that has been given to the letter. However, the contents of the letter indicate that Pauline authorship is most unlikely. The ideas set forth in the letter are not all like the ones found in the genuine letters of Paul. In fact they set forth an interpretation of Christianity that in many respects is foreign to the thought and work of the apostle.

Whoever the author may have been we can be certain that it was someone who believed that Christianity was something more than just another religious movement. He was convinced that it was the only true religion and he wanted to show its superiority over all the ones that were competing with it. He was especially anxious to show its superiority over Judaism. To do this he makes a series of comparisons between conceptions which he finds in the Old Testament and corresponding ideas in his interpretation of Christianity. In each of these instances the Christian view is presented as the more advantageous of the two.

The letter begins with the statement that God, who in ancient times revealed himself through the prophets, has in these last days revealed himself through the life and teachings of a Son. This Son who is identified with the person known as Jesus of Nazareth is said to be greater than Moses or any of the prophets. He is superior even to the angels of heaven for no one of them has ever been called a Son nor did any of them have a part in the creation of the world. Since the message delivered by angels has been valid and any transgression with reference to it has been justly punished, it is all the more important that people should heed what has been delivered to them by the Son. Calling Jesus the Son of God does not, for the author of this letter, constitute a denial of his humanity. On this point he is quite emphatic. "Since therefore the children share in flesh and blood, he himself likewise partook of the same nature." And again "therefore he had to be made like his brethren in every respect." It was because of this that it could be said of Jesus that "he was tempted in all points like as we are" and his victory is therefore able to help all those who are tempted.

Throughout the letter Jesus is referred to as the great high priest whose ministry exceeds in importance the services performed by the priests of ancient Israel. The greatness of the priesthood of Jesus is emphasized in a number of different ways. One of these has to do with the priesthood of Melchizedek. Here the author refers to a story in the book of Genesis concerning Abraham's encounter with Melchizedek who was a priest as well as the king of Salem. Abraham who was returning from the field of battle received a blessing from Melchizedek to whom he paid a tithe of all the spoils he had obtained from the battle. This is the substance of the story as it is reported in Genesis but from this meager account a number of conclusions are drawn. One of these is to the effect that what happened to Abraham in this encounter affected the entire Levitical priesthood since they were all present in the loins of Abraham, the father of the Hebrew people. Asserting that it is always the lesser who is blessed by the better, he infers that the Levitical priesthood is necessarily inferior to the priesthood of Melchizedek and since Jesus is a high priest after the order of Melchizedek, he is therefore greater than any of the priests of the Old Testament. Quoting from Psalms 110 he assumes that it was Jesus about whom the statement was made "You are a priest forever after the order of Melchizedek."

Although Jesus is believed to have been a human being with actual flesh and blood, he was also the Son of God insofar as he was the incarnation of the divine *Logos* or spirit of God. It was this aspect of his nature that was eternal and had neither beginning nor end in the processes of time. This enables the author of the letter to draw another comparison between Jesus and the priests of the Old Testament. The narrative in Genesis says nothing concerning the parentage of Melchizedek and from this silence the conclusion is drawn that he had no father or mother "neither beginning of days nor end of life." In other words he was an eternal rather than a temporal being. Now all of the Levitical priests were men who were born and who died but Jesus who was a priest after the order of Melchizedek had eternal life. But this was not the only point that was significant about the priesthood of Jesus. The work which he performed as a priest exceeded in importance that which was carried on by the men who ministered under the Levitical priesthood. One of the reasons given in support of this claim was the fact that the priests of the tribe of Levi had to perform their services at repeated intervals. Even the sacrifice made on the great day of atonement had to be performed once each year. In contrast with this, Jesus as High Priest offered the sacrifice of himself which was done only once but this one sacrifice was sufficient not only for all time to come but even for those who had died prior to the time when the sacrifice was made. Again the real significance of the sacrifice which Jesus made rests not merely on the fact that it was made once rather than repeated at regular intervals but it was qualitatively different from the ones made by the Levitical priests. The difference lies in the fact that their sacrifices involved merely the blood of bulls and of goats while his sacrifice was that of his own blood. By insisting on this difference the author of the letter did not mean to infer that the sacrifices offered in ancient times had no value at all. They did mean something to the people of Israel. His point was that the sacrifice made by Jesus has even greater value and not for the Jews only but for all mankind insofar as they believe in him. In fact the real significance of the entire sacrificial system as set forth in the Old Testament stands in a very definite relation to the death of Jesus on the cross. As this writer sees it these sacrificial offerings were but shadows which pointed toward another and greater sacrifice to be made in the future and apart from which all of their own services would have been in vain.

Pursuing the subject of Jesus' priesthood still further, the author of this letter gives his own explanations concerning the necessity for a new type of priesthood to replace the older one which had been associated with the tribe of Levi. Again it is the question of duration which he regards as important. The office of priest was hereditary among the Levites and when a priest would die it was necessary for him to be replaced by another whose right to the office would be determined by whether he was a descendant from that particular tribe. Since it was generally recognized that Jesus came from the tribe of Judah, one which had not been designated as a tribe from which the priests were to be chosen, it could be inferred that his right to the priesthood was based not on physical descent but "by the power of an endless life." Furthermore, we are told that Jesus' appointment to the priesthood was confirmed by an oath whereas no such oath was used in the appointment of any of the Levitical priests. The author found support for this statement in his interpretation of a passage found in Psalms 110. The passage reads "The Lord has sworn and will not change his mind. You are a priest forever after the order of Melchizedek." Assuming that the Psalmist was referring to Jesus the statement appeared to give added support to the author's conviction concerning the superiority of the Christian priesthood of Jesus.

This conviction is illustrated again in the assertion that the services performed by the Levitical priests were a part of the system referred to as the old covenant. In contrast with them the priesthood of Jesus belongs to the new covenant. Mention of these two covenants is made in a reference to the passage in the book of Jeremiah in which the prophet contrasts the idea of obedience to a set of external laws with the type of conduct which is motivated by the right desires and purposes within the individual. The former constitutes the basis of the old covenant and the latter the basis for the new covenant. The author of the letter to the Hebrews tells us that the imperfections of the Levitical priesthood were due, at least in part, to the attempt made to regulate conduct according to the requirements of the Mosaic law. The failure of this attempt was one of the reasons that made it necessary to have a new and different type of priesthood. This, he holds, was accomplished in the priesthood of Jesus in accordance with which he became a minister of the new covenant.

The work of Jesus as a High Priest is further elaborated in the author's conception of the heavenly sanctuary. He holds that the tabernacle made by Moses and used by the Israelites during their wanderings in the wilderness was a kind of miniature copy of the true tabernacle or sanctuary which exists in heaven. He bases this belief on the statement found in the book of Exodus describing the instruction which God gave to Moses concerning the construction of that tabernacle. The statement reads "Let them make me a sanctuary that I may dwell among them. According to all that I shew thee after the pattern of the tabernacle, and the pattern of all the instruments thereof, even so shall ye make it." The most important service performed by the Levitical High Priest in the ancient tabernacle took place on the day of atonement. That was the time when he entered into the most holy place and sprinkled blood upon the mercy seat of the ark in order to obtain forgiveness for the sins which the people had committed throughout the year. Believing that these services were intended to foreshadow things to come, the work of Jesus as a High Priest is now declared to be the reality which fulfills the meaning intended by the ancient services. Following his resurrection and ascension to heaven Jesus enters into the most holy place in the heavenly sanctuary and there offers his own blood in atonement for the sins of mankind.

These references to the Old Testament are significant because they indicate a belief on the part of the author that it is in the events associated with the life, death, and resurrection of Jesus that the stories related in the Old Testament find their true meaning. Especially is this true with reference to those portions of the Old Testament that have to do with the priests and the sacrificial system of which they were a part. The discussion concerning faith which comes toward the close of this letter is in harmony with this same point of view. Enumerating a long list of Israel's heroes, he maintains that it was by faith that all of their mighty works were accomplished. His conception of faith is then identified with a belief on their part that at some future time the Christ would appear and do those things which have now been accomplished.

Commentary

The letter to the Hebrews holds a unique place in the literature of the New Testament. It presents an interpretation of Jesus and indeed of the entire Christian movement that strikes one as decidedly different from that which is found in the other writings. The author sees Jesus as the great

High Priest of the Christian religion performing services analogous to the ones carried out by the Levitical priests of the Old Testament. In other portions of the New Testament Jesus is regarded as a prophet but it is only in this letter that he is considered a priest. This designation is significant for the prophets usually represented a point of view that in many respects was the very opposite of that of the priests. The prophets were the great social reformers while the priests gave attention to the offering of sacrifices and the performance of ritualistic requirements which were necessary in order to obtain forgiveness of sins. It is true that the work of the priests occupied a very prominent place in the lives of those whose religious heritage was in Judaism. With the destruction of the Temple in Jerusalem and the cessation of priestly activities it seems probable that there were those who felt the need for something to be substituted in their place. It may be that considerations of this kind influenced to some extent the author of this letter. At any rate he interprets the death of Jesus on the cross in a manner that not only meets the requirements of Judaism but goes beyond them.

The use of the Old Testament which one finds in this letter has led some people to refer to Hebrews as the classical example of the New Testament interpretation of the Old Testament. It illustrates the tendency on the part of some Christians to read their own ideas back into the literature of the ancient people of Israel. Having arrived at certain convictions concerning the meaning and significance of the life of Jesus, they assume that these same ideas were present in the minds of those who wrote the Old Testament. When this has been done, it becomes a fairly easy task to find in their writings the very ideas for which they are looking. Apparently this is what the author of the letter to the Hebrews did in many of the instances which occur in his writings. This is especially true of his references to the sacrificial system of the Levitical priests and of the passages which refer to the priesthood of Melchizedek. In the synoptic gospels as well as in other portions of the New Testament reference is made to the Messianic prophecies of the Old Testament. In Hebrews no reference is made to these prophecies. Instead it is the sacrificial offerings that were made by the priests which anticipated the coming of Jesus and his death on the cross. This way of looking at the Old Testament has had an important bearing on the development of Christian doctrine. It had led in some instances to the view that the Old Testament was really a Christian rather than a Jewish book. The people for whom it was written did not understand it and it is only in the light of Christian beliefs that its true meaning can be discerned. The most extreme statement of this position is expressed in the words of one Christian writer who maintained that "the Old Testament is but the New Testament concealed and the New Testament is the Old Testament revealed."

The influence of this letter to the Hebrews is reflected again in many of the generally accepted teachings of the Christian church. One of these is the doctrine of the blood atonement or the idea that it was the blood of Jesus which atones for or pays the penalty for human transgressions. Likewise the interpretation of the faith by which men are saved as being identical with the mere belief that Jesus died for the sins of the world has sometimes been supported by quotations from this letter. This is not to say that the author of the letter believed that Christian faith involved no more than this, but rather that some of the specific things he did say have in many instances suggested this interpretation.

Aside from these peculiarities there are several other ideas which must be taken into account in forming one's estimation of the value of the letter taken as a whole. The statement that Jesus was one who "reflects the glory of God and who bears the very stamp of his nature" explains the relationship between Jesus and the Father in a most meaningful way. The humanity of Jesus is emphasized in the assertion that "he was tempted in all points like as we are," and again that he was "one who was made perfect through suffering." Since the letter was addressed to those who were becoming discouraged and growing weak in the faith, the messages which it conveyed were both comforting and reassuring.

THE REVELATION OF JOHN

Summary

It is in the *Revelation of John* that the apocalyptic hopes of the early Christian community found its clearest and most complete expression. Apocalypticism was not a new phenomenon among the Christians. It had been for a long time a well established belief among the Jews who held that the coming of the kingdom of God would not be brought about by a gradual transformation but by a sudden intervention when God would bring an end to the present age and establish his kingdom in the world made new. This conception of coming events was associated with the belief that prior to this time the struggle between the forces of good and evil would become more intense. The evil powers would become stronger and as they did so they would inflict persecution and in some instances even death upon those who were following a course of righteousness. The struggle would eventually reach a climax at which time God would intervene, destroy the forces of evil, and set up a new order of things in which the righteous would live for all time to come. It was generally believed that the appearance of the Messiah would coincide with the coming of these events.

When the members of the Christian community affirmed their belief that the man Jesus who had been crucified was the long awaited Messiah it was necessary for them to revise their understanding concerning the work he was to do and especially the way in which it would be carried on to completion. Because they were convinced that the work of the Messiah must end in triumph and in glory, it seemed to them that this end could be accomplished only by a return of Jesus from the heaven to which he had ascended back to this earth. This second coming would occur at the time when all the events connected with the apocalyptic program would take place. It would inaugurate the coming of the new age, as well as the final destruction of all the forces of evil.

As time went on, many of the Christians became deeply concerned about how long it would be before these events would take place. This was especially true of the ones who were suffering persecution at the hands of the Roman government. Toward the end of the first century of the Christian era, emperor worship had become fairly well established not only in the city of Rome but in the colonies which formed a part of the empire. When the Christians refused to worship the emperor they were accused of all sorts of crimes and subjected to the most severe penalties. Some of them suffered martyrdom rather than deny their faith. It was a critical time for the entire Christian movement. Many of its members wondered whether the persecution would ever end. Others were perplexed about the course they should follow. Some were tempted to abandon the faith or at least to make concessions to Rome sufficient to enable them to save their lives. It was under these conditions that a Christian named John wrote the *Revelation* or *Apocalypse* addressing it to the seven churches that were in Asia Minor. The purpose of the book was to strengthen the faith of the members of these churches by giving to them the assurance that deliverance from the evil powers arrayed against them was close at hand. He was confident that the great day when divine intervention would take place would occur within a comparatively short time, but in accordance with the apocalyptic literature with which the Christians of Jewish heritage were all familiar he knew that many terrifying events would take place first. He wanted to warn his fellow Christians concerning these events and thus prepare them for the time when their faith would be put to a more severe test than anything which they had experienced thus far.

In the writing of this book John followed the pattern which had been used in the older apocalyptic writings such as the book of *Daniel* in the Old Testament, the book called *I Esdras* in the Apocrypha, the book of *Enoch* in the Pseudepigrapha, the *Assumption of Moses,* and many other well known writings including sections in the book of *Ezekiel* and portions of the synoptic gospels. In all of these writings it was made to appear that events had been predicted long before they actually took place. The revelations were usually made through dreams or visions in which coming events were symbolized by strange figures the meaning of which would sometimes be disclosed by an angelic messenger who would be sent for that particular purpose. The apocalypses were always produced in a time of crisis and they were written for the benefit of those who were suffering hardship and privation at the particular time when the writing was done.

At the beginning of the book John tells us he was on the Isle of Patmos where he had been banished because of his religious faith. While "in the Spirit on the Lord's Day" he heard a loud voice telling him to write what he saw in a book and send it to the seven churches in Asia. The voice was that of Jesus the Christ, the one who had been raised from the dead and who had ascended to heaven. The messages are addressed to the seven angels, each one of which is the guardian for a particular church. The churches named are *Ephesus, Smyrna, Thyatira, Pergamum, Sardis, Philadelphia,* and *Laodicea.* To all of these there is given a word of commendation for the good works which they have performed but for five of them there is also a message of warning and reproof. John is especially critical of those who tolerate the doctrines of the Nicolaitans. He considers their teachings a real menace to the Christian community because they approve of the practice of eating meat which has been obtained from animals that have been used as a sacrifice to idols. It is true that the Apostle Paul and other Christians had maintained that this was not a matter of vital importance and with reference to it everyone should be permitted to follow the dictates of his own conscience. But apparently John did not share this attitude. As he understood it, the crucial test for all Christians as it had been for Jews, was strict obedience to all the laws that had been required of them and the rules pertaining to the kinds of food that were forbidden were no exception. Even though it might appear to be relatively unimportant, one's attitude toward matters of this kind would indicate the way in which they would behave toward weightier matters. Special commendation is given to those churches whose members have endured persecution and in some instances even death rather than to declare their allegiance to the Roman rulers who have proclaimed their own divinity and demanded that they too should be worshipped along with the other gods of the empire. John refers to *Pergamon* as Satan's home or headquarters, inasmuch as it was in this place that the cult of emperor worship was particularly strong. The instruction given to the Christians is to the effect that they may expect their persecutions will be even more severe in the immediate future. Nevertheless they are to remain faithful, regarding these afflictions as tests of their character. Those who remain loyal to the end will not only be delivered from the hands of their enemies but in the new order of things that will soon be established they will be given a crown of life and the assurance that it will last forever. The persecutions which are now taking place will last for only a short time, for the hour of God's judgment is close at hand.

Following the messages to the seven churches, John describes the seven seals. These are scrolls on which there is written an account of the events which are about to take place. The risen Christ who is referred to as the Lamb of God is said to be the only one who is accounted worthy to open the seals. The first seal is opened and there appears a white horse whose rider goes forth conquering and to conquer. Other seals are opened and there appears in rapid succession three more horses, a red one, a black one, and a pale one. These four horses and their respective riders symbolize the conflicts which will mark the beginning of the final destruction of the Roman empire. When the fifth seal is opened John is permitted to look upon the souls of those who in the midst of their distress cry out "how long must this continue?" They are told that the forces of destruction are about to be turned loose in the world and they may have to endure even greater torment but if they are faithful through it all they will be among the redeemed whose names are all written in the book of life.

Following John's vision of the impending disasters soon to be inflicted upon the world, the scene changes and the four angels representing the four winds of heaven are told to hold back these winds until the servants of God are sealed in their foreheads. He then reveals the number of those who are sealed. Drawing an analogy between the twelve tribes of ancient Israel and the Christian community regarded now as the new Israel he gives the number of 144,000, which is 12,000 from each of the tribes of Israel. Before the opening of the seals is completed another series of disasters is revealed in the appearance of seven angels, each one of which is carrying a trumpet in his hand. The blowing of these trumpets announces the coming of physical disturbances such as the coming of a great earthquake, the turning of rivers into blood and the darkening of the sun and the moon as well as the falling of the stars from heaven. After these physical phenomena which will indeed be appalling, the wrath of God will be visited more directly upon those who have persecuted the members of the Christian community. Before describing the manner of this visitation, John identifies the power now vested in the Roman emperor with the evil one, who through the centuries has been at war with the forces that make for righteousness.

This evil one is none other than Satan the arch enemy of God who is now putting forth a supreme effort to destroy the righteous from the face of the earth. He is the Dragon who launched a rebellion against God before he came to earth. John tells us "there was war in heaven" as Michael and his angels fought against the Dragon and his angels. The result of the conflict was that the Dragon was cast out of heaven and a third of the angels were cast out with him. It was the same Dragon that worked through king Herod in an attempt to destroy the Christ child as soon as he was born. His work has continued ever since and as John sees it he is now trying to accomplish his purpose by working through the Roman emperor. His evil character is now manifest in the cruel persecutions which are being inflicted upon the Christians. In characterizing this power which now appears to be gaining mastery over the world, John resorts to the imagery which was used in the book of Daniel to describe the wicked ruler who tried to coerce the Jews into submission. The author of the book of Daniel had used the symbol of a great and terrible beast that had seven heads and ten horns. In like manner John uses "the beast and his image" to represent the Roman emperor whose image was stamped on the coins that were used in the empire. At one point he becomes quite specific in his identification of the one symbolized by the beast. He says "Here is wisdom, let him that hath understanding count the number of the beast for it is the number of a man, and his number is six hundred three score and six." Since the Roman letters were used at times to represent numbers, and the numerical value of the letters used to designate the emperor equals this amount it would seem that John is referring to this particular individual. But it is also evident that he is personifying the forces of evil and his condemnation of the emperor is due to the fact that he believes Satan is incarnate in the actions of the empire and they are linked together for the achievement of a common purpose.

As John sees the end drawing near, he describes the angels of heaven crying with a loud voice "Woe, woe, woe, unto the inhabitants of the earth." Following this proclamation seven angels appear each one carrying a bowl the contents of which symbolize the wrath of God about to be poured out in the form of the seven last plagues. The plagues will be inflicted upon the wicked of John's day just as a series of plagues fell upon the ancient Egyptians prior to the time when the Israelites were delivered from their bondage. When the first angel pours out his bowl upon the earth, foul and evil sores come upon the men who bear the mark of the beast and who worship his image. When the second one pours out his bowl on the sea it turns to blood and everything living in it dies. Catastrophes of a similar nature follow when the remaining angels empty their bowls. After this three more angels appear, the first one announcing that the hour of God's judgment has come; the second one crying out that Babylon which is used as the symbol of Rome is fallen; and the third one describing the terrible fate of those who worship the beast or his image. As a final punishment they are thrown into a lake of fire where they will forever be destroyed.

The great catastrophic events which bring an end to all the kingdoms of earth will also be the occasion for the return of Christ upon the clouds of heaven. As he approaches the earth the wicked people will all be slain by the brightness of his coming. Then for a period of a thousand years Satan will be bound and the earth will be desolate. During this time the righteous will be made safe in the city of God which is the New Jerusalem. At the end of the thousand years, the city of God will descend to earth. Then the wicked will be raised from the dead and after making an attempt to overthrow the city of God they will be destroyed in what John tells us is the second death. The closing chapters of the book present a glowing description of the new Jerusalem with its streets of gold, its walls of jasper, its gates of pearl and the river of Life which will flow eternally from the throne of God. In this heavenly abode there will be neither sorrow nor crying for God will wipe away all tears, and there will be no more death.

Commentary

The *Revelation of John* is the one book in the New Testament which claims John as its author. By the time the writings which are now included in our New Testament were assembled in their present form, three letters and one gospel were also attributed to John. But in the case of these writings the name of the supposed author was added at a later date, and their respective contents indicate that it was not the same John who wrote the Revelation. The Revelation of John has often been regarded as a mysterious book quite beyond the comprehension of the average lay reader. Its many references to angelic beings, its elaborate description of Christ as he appears in the heavenly courts, its use of such mystic numbers as three, seven, twelve, and their multiples, the account of strange beasts, symbolic names, and definite time periods, all suggest some hidden and esoteric meaning which can be detected only by an expert. For these reasons many persons have ignored the book, feeling that any attempt to understand it would be futile. Other persons have taken an opposite attitude and have found in this book what they believe to have been predictions of whole series of events, many of which have already occurred and the remainder are about to take place in the near future. The basis for these views, many of which sound strange and fantastic, is found in the elaborate symbolism used in the book. It is true that the use of symbols has an important place in religious literature for there is no other way in which one can talk or even think about that which goes beyond the realm of finite human experience. But there is always a danger that the symbols may be interpreted in a way that was not intended by the author who used them. It is only in the light of the content in which the symbols were used that one can determine what the author meant.

One source of confusion has been the result of a failure to distinguish between prophetic writing and apocalyptic writing. The prophets used a particular literary form in which they expressed their messages. The apocalyptic writers used a different literary form, one that was more suited to the particular purpose which they had in mind. To understand either group one must interpret their writings in the light of the respective literary form that was used. The characteristics of apocalyptic writing are fairly well known at the present time. In addition to the books of *Daniel* and the *Revelation* which are a part of the Bible there is a wealth of apocalyptic writing in the books of the *Apocrypha* and the *Pseudepigrapha* of the Old Testament. A careful study of these writings shows that they have a number of common characteristics. They are produced in times of crises, they describe the conflict between the forces of good and evil, future events are made known through dreams and visions, the end of the conflict is to come shortly, and those who remain faithful through persecutions and trial are promised a reward in the messianic kingdom soon to be established. The messages are for the benefit of the ones being tried and they are usually conveyed by means of symbols which only the faithful would understand.

Interpreted in the light of these characteristics the *Revelation of John* is comparatively easy to understand. In many respects it is the least original of any of the New Testament writings. In its style of writing, the number and kind of symbols that are used, and the purpose for which it was written, the book follows closely the precedent that had been established in the older apocalyptic writings. The unique feature about it is the particular occasion which caused it to be written. Toward the end of the first century of the Christian era, the attitude of the Roman government toward Christianity became especially hostile. Nero, the Roman emperor had charged that the Christians were to blame for the burning of Rome. Although the charge was false it was sufficient to cause many people to regard the new movement with suspicion. Jews and Romans alike resented the fact that Christians condemned so many of the things they were doing. They especially disliked the belief on the part of Christians that their religion was superior to the older faiths that had been honored for centuries. The Christians often held their meetings in secret places and their critics imagined they were doing all sorts of evil things. It was easy to circulate rumors of this kind and along with other things they were charged with plotting against the Roman government. As the opposition to Christianity became more intense, the followers of the new movement were asked to prove their loyalty to the Roman government by denouncing Christ and by worshipping the statue of the Emperor. When they refused to do this they were often tortured or even put to death.

It was under these conditions that the *Revelation of John* was written. It would be difficult to imagine anything more appropriate for the members of Christian churches at that time. They needed encouragement and the assurance that their trials would soon be over, the evil powers of the earth destroyed, and the triumph of righteousness established in the world. The message of the book was intended for that particular time and set of circumstances. Christians who were familiar with the older apocalyptic writings would understand the symbolism used, for practically everything John had to say to his contemporaries had been said before to people who had suffered under similar circumstances. It is a mistake to suppose that John was predicting events that would take place in the later centuries of Christian history. He was writing to the people of his own day about events that would happen while they were still living. He states that Christ will return while those who put him to death on the cross are still living. The permanent significance of the book lies in the author's conviction that right will ultimately triumph over evil.

THE GOSPEL OF JOHN

Summary

The *Gospel of John* is the latest of the four biographies of Jesus that have been preserved in the New Testament. It was written by a Christian who bore the name of John but the contents of the book indicate quite clearly that the author was not the John who was one of the twelve disciples of Jesus. It contains no direct personal references of the type one would expect from an intimate associate. On the contrary it presents an interpretation of Jesus that reflects ideas and situations which prevailed in the Christian community toward the end of the first century of the Christian era. This was a time when Christianity was under attack from several different quarters. Jews, Romans skeptics and others were making charges against it. The author of this Gospel was evidently aware of these attacks and he knew too that some of the accounts given in the earlier Gospels had been interpreted in a manner which seemed to support some of these charges. Because he believed so firmly in the new Christian movement he wanted to write a gospel that would set forth its essential truth in the best possible manner. It was his hope that he might write one that would not only be true to the facts but which would at the same time offer a presentation of the Christian faith that would overcome the objections of its critics and gain the respect of the educated and cultured people of his day. This objective helps us to understand many of the unique characteristics of his gospel especially the ones which are in sharp contrast with the synoptic gospels. It explains, for one thing, the omission in the

Gospel of John of so many items found in the earlier accounts. It also explains, at least in part, the different attitude expressed concerning the Jews, the allegorical interpretation given of certain miracle stories, the absence of apocalypticism with reference to the second coming, the subordinate role of John the Baptist, the new concept of the Messiah, and many other peculiarities of this gospel.

The purpose of this gospel, as stated by the author himself was to show that Jesus of Nazareth was the Christ, the Son of God, and that by believing in him men might have eternal life. This purpose was one which John had in common with the men who wrote the synoptic gospels but his method for achieving it was what distinguished his gospel from the ones they had written. The central theme in the synoptic gospels had been the coming of the kingdom of God and it was in relation to this event that an account had been given of the life and teachings of Jesus. The Messianic character of his mission had been described in terms of the miracles which he performed, his kindly attitude toward the poor and the oppressed, his power to cast out demons and to heal the sick, and his instructions concerning the way men should live in view of the imminence of the coming kingdom.

In the *Gospel of John* the central theme is the divine *Logos,* the word which was with God and which was God. It was this *Logos* that became flesh and dwelt among men and it was in the person of Jesus of Nazareth that this took place. John says nothing of a supernatural birth. He regards Jesus as a human being who possessed actual flesh and blood the same as other people. The most significant thing about Jesus was the fact that the divine *Logos* was present in him and all of the marvelous things which he did were accomplished by virtue of the power of God. It is in this way that John conceives the relationship between the divine and the human. Because God was present in Jesus, it was appropriate to refer to him as the Son of God but this was regarded as an example of what can happen in the life of anyone else in whom the power of God dwells. It is in this connection that John says "to as many as believed on him, to them gave he the power to become sons of God."

John's account of the ministry of Jesus consists of two parts. The first twelve chapters describe his public ministry which begins with his meeting with John the Baptist and closes with the visit of the Greeks who had come to worship at the feast of the Passover. The remaining chapters have to do with the closing days of his ministry in which he gives instruction to his disciples and explains the meaning of his life and approaching death in a number of lengthy discourses. This division of the gospel into two parts follows the pattern used by the synoptic writers but the content of the two sections differs widely from the earlier accounts. According to John, Jesus' public ministry can be summarized in connection with a number of miracles which are reported and followed by interpretations which point to their spiritual significance.

John records only seven miracles which is considerably less than the number reported in the synoptic gospels. But John's use of the miracle stories is different from that of his predecessors. It is not the miraculous element in the story that John regards as having great significance but rather the spiritual meaning which he finds implicit in them. They are "signs" not of the imminence of the coming of the kingdom as that term is used in the synoptic gospels, but of the presence of the *Logos* or the power of God which brings about a transformation in men's lives.

The seven "signs" or miracle stories recorded in John are, first, the turning of water into wine at the marriage feast in Cana; second, the healing of the nobleman's son who was at the point of death; third, the healing of the man at the sheep-gate pool; fourth, walking on the water; fifth, the feeding of five thousand; sixth, the healing of the man born blind; and seventh, the raising of Lazarus. Each of these stories is used as a kind of introduction to a discourse concerning the significance of Jesus and his message in relation to the quality of one's living. This use of the miracle stories for the purpose of teaching spiritual lessons is made possible by analogies and in many instances an allegorizing of the materials found in the story. For example, the story about Jesus turning the water into wine is interpreted to mean the contrast between the old and the new dispensations. The water in the story symbolizes a cleansing and the transformation which takes place when one's life is filled with the Spirit that was present in Jesus, stands in sharp contrast with the rites and ceremonies performed in the Jewish Temple. This meaning of the story is given special emphasis in the narratives which follow. In one of these Jesus drives out the buyers and sellers from the Temple. In the synoptic gospels this event is placed toward the close of Jesus' ministry but John puts it toward the beginning because to him it represents the purpose or goal of his entire earthly career. He quotes Jesus as saying "Destroy this Temple and in three days I will raise it up." This is a reference to John's belief that in the death and resurrection of Jesus a new and more meaningful conception of salvation has been brought about. The point is illustrated even further in the story of the conversation with Nicodemus in which Jesus talks about the necessity of the new birth and says that unless one is born of the water and the spirit he cannot see the kingdom of God. The same point of view is expressed again in the account of Jesus' conversation with the woman at the well of

Samaria. In reply to her questions concerning the proper place and manner of worship he explained that what is most important is not the external forms which one observes but they who really worship the Father must do so "in spirit and in truth."

The story of the feeding of the five thousand appears to have been taken from the synoptic gospels where it was presented as evidence that Jesus was the Messiah because he had power to work miracles. John reports the story as it was customarily understood but the use which he makes of it is quite different from that of the earlier writers. For John it was not the amount of physical food that came into existence that was of primary importance. Instead it was the meaning of the story in relation to the spiritual food which alone can sustain the quality of living which characterizes the true followers of Jesus. Accordingly, the account of the miracles is followed immediately by a discourse in which Jesus says "I am the Bread of Life." In an obvious reference to the practice of Christians in celebrating the Eucharist or Lord's Supper, John quotes Jesus as saying "He who eats my flesh and drinks my blood has eternal life." It is the presence of the *Logos* or spirit of God in human life that really nourishes the spiritual quality of one's living. Just as Jesus, by virtue of this spirit, gives the living water that brings eternal life, so he gives the food that can bring a new quality of life to the world.

When Jesus heals the man who was born blind, the people who witnessed the miracle had inquired "who sinned, this man or his parents that he was born blind?" In reply it was said "Neither this man nor his parents but in order that the power of God might be made manifest." The discussion which follows makes it clear that John's major concern in this narrative was not physical sight in place of physical blindness but rather the curing of men and women of their spiritual blindness. Those who had failed to understand Jesus and the purpose of his mission in the world were spiritually blind. Only by coming under the influence of his spirit could they pass from darkness into light.

It is in the story of the resurrection of Lazarus, the brother of Mary and Martha, that John's interpretation of the signs reaches its climax. Lazarus has been dead for four days and at the call of Jesus he comes back to life. An event of this kind is for John a most appropriate symbol of what happens to people who are spiritually dead when they are receptive to the power of God which was made manifest in the person of Jesus. The fact that this story is found only in the Gospel of John raises some questions concerning the historicity of the event, for it does not seem at all probable that the authors of the synoptic gospels would have failed to relate an event as important as this one if they had known about it. Whether John was recording a popular tradition or writing a sequel to the story of the rich man and Lazarus, recorded in the Gospel of Luke, we do not know. At any rate the story in Luke closes with the statement that those who do not believe Moses and the prophets would not be convinced even though one who had been raised from the dead should speak to them. In John's story, someone does come from the dead and even then the Jews are not persuaded by what has been said or done. As John interprets the story its deeper meaning is disclosed in the statement which Jesus makes "I am the resurrection and the life; he who believes in me, though he die yet shall he live, and whoever lives and believes in me shall never die." Lazarus is typical of all men. Without the indwelling presence of the spirit of God all human life is meaningless. It is when this spirit enters into their lives that they are no longer dead in a spiritual sense but are partakers of the life which is everlasting.

The remaining portions of the Gospel of John record incidents that are closely related to the closing days of Jesus' ministry. Unlike the Gospel of Mark the story of the anointing of Jesus by Mary is placed before instead of after the triumphal entry into Jerusalem, and the Passover meal with the disciples is said to have taken place one day earlier than in the account given in the Synoptic Gospels. These changes were quite in harmony with John's conception of Jesus as "the lamb of God who takes away the sins of the world." Since the paschal lamb used as a sacrifice by the ancient Jews was always slain on the day before the Passover it seemed most appropriate to John that the sacrifice of Jesus should be in conformity with the ancient tradition.

The major emphasis in this part of John's Gospel is to be found in the discourses which are attributed to Jesus. Because John is interpreting the meaning of Jesus' earthly career from the perspective of the post-resurrection experiences and beliefs of the Christian community these discourses are presented as though they had been made in anticipation of the events which had followed. This can be seen in the story of the foot-washing which preceded the eating of the Passover meal. By performing the work of a servant Jesus not only gave to his disciples an example of humility which they were to follow but the water used in the service was a symbol of that spiritual cleansing which was essential for all those who became true followers of him. This was the meaning of the statement made to Peter "If I wash thee not, thou hast no part with me." And when Jesus said to the group of disciples "Ye are clean but not all" he was referring to Judas who was about to betray him as he left the room in a state of spiritual blindness and went out to make contact with the enemies of Jesus.

In one of the discourses Jesus explained his relation to the Father by using the parable of the vine and the branches. He showed in what sense it was true that the Son and the Father were one. They were one in spirit and in purpose without either of them losing their personal identity. The Father works through the Son for the redemption of the world but the task is one that must be continued after the earthly career of the Son has ended. It is in this connection that Jesus speaks of going to the Father in order that the Comforter or Spirit of God may be present in the hearts and minds of the believers and thus continue through the church the work which he had been doing while dwelling in their midst. This is John's version of the second coming. It replaces at least in part, the apocalyptic expectations which are present in all three of the synoptic gospels. John, no less than the synoptic writers, believes that some day the forces of evil in this world will be overcome and God's reign of righteousness will be finally established. But instead of it being brought about by a sudden catastrophic event which will bring to an end the nations of the world, and at which time Jesus will return to earth in power and great glory, John sees the return of Jesus whenever and wherever the Spirit of God enters into the lives of human beings. He believes it is the function of the Christian church to follow the guidance and direction of this spirit until the whole world has been transformed into a kingdom of God.

In a long and remarkable prayer which John attributes to Jesus the meaning and significance of his entire career is neatly summarized. We may be sure that the language used is that of John rather than Jesus for it contains the same type of statements which are used throughout the gospels and there are places where Jesus is referred to in the third person. But this is a relatively unimportant item. The fact is that the prayer contains what John believes to be implicit in the life and teaching of Jesus. It is a fitting resume, as he sees it, of what Jesus has done for the Christian community and indeed for all those who at any future time will become members of it. The Christian community, at the time when John wrote, was experiencing a great deal of opposition not only from the Jews but from the Romans and others who were skeptical of the claims which Christians were making. At times this opposition led to severe persecution and there were those who wanted to withdraw from direct contact with the people of the world. It was to these persons that the words of Jesus were addressed "I pray not that you be taken out of the world but that you might be saved from the evil that is in the world." Following the prayer, John describes the events which culminated in the crucifixion of Jesus. He reports the words which Jesus uttered while on the cross. The last of these "It is finished" carries a double meaning, for they indicated not only that Jesus was about to die but that the whole purpose of the incarnation was now complete. The

Gospel closes with an account of the post-resurrection experiences which took place both in Jerusalem and in Galilee.

Commentary

The importance of this gospel can scarcely be overestimated. Throughout Christian history it has been read and cherished far more than any of the other accounts of Jesus' life that have been preserved. The language used is simple enough that it can be read and appreciated by the poor and uneducated and yet the ideas expressed are so profound that they appeal to the most cultured and highly educated classes of people. The genius of the gospel lies in the way in which the author conceives of the relationship between the human and the divine. This has always been a problem which has puzzled the minds of thoughtful persons. How can God who is conceived as an eternal, omniscient, and omnipotent being have any direct contact with that which is temporal, changing, and limited by the conditions of space and time? In other words, how can divinity ever be united with humanity unless one thereby becomes involved in a contradiction of terms? John's answer to this question is his statement that "The Word became flesh and dwelt among men." The Logos is identified with God and this is the spirit which dwelt in the human being known as Jesus of Nazareth. It was this divine spirit which motivated his activities and which enabled him to meet triumphantly the temptations to which all human beings are subject. As John sees it, no human being can in his own strength overcome the forces of evil in even his own life. It is only God who can impart to human beings the power to do this. The fact that it was done in the person of Jesus is all the evidence that is needed to assure to men everywhere that triumph over evil is a possibility for them too, and that the ultimate overthrow of the forces of evil is something that has now been made certain.

Throughout John's Gospel, Jesus appears in the role of a human being and this is especially important because it means that he is an example for other people to follow. As a typical human being he possessed no extraordinary power which is not available to anyone else who asks for it and who meets the conditions for receiving it. Because his will is in complete harmony with the will of God it is proper and right to refer to him as the Son of God and it is in this connection that we are to understand the statement "To as many as believed on Him, to them gave he the power to become Sons of God."

John's treatment of the miracle stories is especially significant. In the synoptic gospels the purpose of the miracle appears to be that of presenting evidence to support the claim that Jesus was the true Messiah. The evidence consisted in the ability to do that which ordinary human beings could not do. In this case the historical accuracy of the event as reported would be crucial. In John's gospel only seven miracles are reported and in no one of these instances is the real meaning of the story dependent on its historical accuracy. This is not to say that John has any doubts about their historical accuracy. He does not discuss that point for he has something else in mind that he regards as far more important. It is the spiritual lesson that he derives from it and this lesson would be exactly the same whether the details of the story are reported accurately or not. One of the advantages of the Gospel of John is that it presents the meaning of Christianity in a way that makes its validity dependent on neither scientific accuracy nor historical verification. This position is a fortunate one for the modern world since we have no adequate means for determining exactly what happened in regard to any of the reported events. All of the evidence we have is what the individuals who made the records believed to have happened.

The interpretation of Christianity set forth in this gospel may be characterized as mystical in the same sense that the Pauline letters are mystical. In both instances the essence of salvation is the mystical union of the human and the divine. It was the presence of God in the life of Jesus of Nazareth that enabled him to overcome the temptations which arise from contact with the flesh and the world, and it is this same presence of the divine Spirit of God which can enter into the heart and life of any individual who believes in him and who will allow this spirit to become the motivating force in his life. Paul had expressed this conception in the words "I live and yet not I; it is Christ who lives and who abides in me." John says that just as the branch cannot bear fruit except it abides in the vine, so the Christian cannot live the good life unless Christ abides within him. This type of mysticism unites the believer with God and yet it does so without destroying the individuality of either. It is in this respect that Christian mysticism differs from those types in which individual personality is destroyed by becoming wholly absorbed in the deity.

A SELECTED BIBLIOGRAPHY

Baillie, D. M.   *God Was in Christ*
                    Charles Scribner's Sons, N. Y. 1948

Baillie, John   *The Idea of Revelation in Recent Thought*
                    Columbia University Press, N. Y. 1956

Barclay, William   *The Mind of St. Paul*
Harper & Bros. N. Y. 1958

Bornkamm, Gunther   *Jesus of Nazareth*
Harper & Bros. N. Y. 1956

Crownfield, F. R.   *A Historical Approach to the New Testament*
Harper & Bros. N. Y. 1960

Eakin, Frank   *Getting Acquainted with the New Testament*
Macmillan Co. N. Y. 1927

Feris, Theodore P.   *The Image of God*
Oxford University Press, N. Y. 1965

Fosdick, Harry E.   *The Man from Nazareth*
Harper & Bros. N. Y. 1949

Kee and Young   *Understanding the New Testament*
Prentice-Hall, Englewood Cliffs, N. J. 1965

Niles, A. J.   *As Seeing the Invisible*
Harper & Bros, N. Y. 1961

Price, James L.   *Interpreting the New Testament*
Holt, Rinehart and Winston, N. Y. 1961

Pfeiffer, Robert   *A History of New Testament Times*
Harper & Bros. N. Y. 1949

Titus, Eric L.   *Essentials of New Testament Study*
Ronald Press, N. Y. 1958

NOTES

Study Smart with Cliffs StudyWare®

Cliffs StudyWare is interactive software that helps you make the most of your study time. The programs are easy to use and designed to let you work at your own pace.

Test Preparation Guides—
Prepare for major qualifying exams.
• Pinpoint strengths and weaknesses through individualized study plan. • Learn more through complete answer explanations. • Hone your skills with full-length practice tests. • Score higher by utilizing proven test-taking strategies.

Course Reviews—Designed for introductory college level courses.
• Supplement class lectures and textbook reading. • Review for midterms and finals.

Qty.	Title		Price	Total	Qty.	Title		Price	Total
	Algebra I	☐ IBM ☐ Mac	19.98			Statistics	☐ IBM ☐ Mac	19.98	
	Algebra I CD-ROM (IBM & Mac)		24.98			Trigonometry (TMV)	☐ IBM ☐ Mac	19.98	
	Biology	☐ IBM ☐ Mac	19.98			ACT	☐ IBM ☐ Mac	19.98	
	Biology CD-ROM (IBM & Mac)		24.98			ACT CD-ROM (IBM & Mac)		24.98	
	Calculus	☐ IBM ☐ Mac	19.98			CBEST	☐ IBM ☐ Mac	19.98	
	Calculus CD-ROM (IBM & Mac)		24.98			College Bound Bndl. (ACT, SAT, U.S. News)		29.98	
	Chemistry	☐ IBM ☐ Mac	19.98			GED	☐ IBM ☐ Mac	19.98	
	Chemistry CD-ROM (IBM & Mac)		24.98			GMAT	☐ IBM ☐ Mac	19.98	
	Economics	☐ IBM ☐ Mac	19.98			GRE	☐ IBM ☐ Mac	19.98	
	Geometry	☐ IBM ☐ Mac	19.98			GRE CD-ROM (IBM & Mac)		24.98	
	Geometry CD-ROM (IBM & Mac)		24.98			LSAT	☐ IBM ☐ Mac	19.98	
	Math Bundle (Alg., Calc., Geom., Trig.)		39.98			SAT I	☐ IBM ☐ Mac	19.98	
	Physics	☐ IBM ☐ Mac	19.98			SAT I CD-ROM (IBM & Mac)		24.98	

Prices subject to change without notice.

Available at your booksellers, or send this form with your check or money order to **Cliffs Notes, Inc., P.O. Box 80728, Lincoln, NE 68501** http://www.cliffs.com

Get the Cliffs Edge!

☐ Money order ☐ Check payable to Cliffs Notes, Inc.

☐ Visa ☐ Mastercard Signature _____

Card no. _____ Exp. date _____

Name _____

Address _____

City _____ State _____ Zip _____

GRE is a registered trademark of ETS. SAT is a registered trademark of CEEB.